Gourmet & Delicious

QUICK YUMMY MEALS

Mediterranean Diet Cookbook for Two Made Simple

Healthy, Easy, Quick Meals in 15 minutes or Less

Sherri Todd

Gourmet & Delicious

Copyright @2024 by Sherri Todd

FIRST EDITION

Your Feedback is Greatly Appreciated!

It's through your feedback, support and reviews that I'm able to create the best books possible and serve more people.

I would be extremely grateful if you could take just 60 seconds to kindly leave an honest review of the book on Amazon. Please share your feedback and thoughts for others to see.

To do so, simply find the book on Amazon's website (or wherever you purchased the book from) and locate the section to leave a review. Select a star rating and write a couple of sentences.

That's it! Thank you so much for your support.

Click with your camera above to get a free e-book: "Mediterranean Diet Program: Healthy Effective Weight Loss" or copy/type in
bit.ly/3YMcAr7

Table of Contents

Free Book 4

Table of Content 13

Introduction.. 19

Overview of the Mediterranean Diet... 21

The History of the Mediterranean Diet 22

The Key Components of the Mediterranean Diet 23

The Mediterranean Diet Food Pyramid................................... 24

Health Benefits of the Mediterranean Diet 25

Tip and Tricks for Mediterranean Diet 29

How to Start.. 29

Cooking Tips for Two 31

Food to Eat and Avoid.. 33

Breakfast... 37

1.   Orange Cardamom Buckwheat Pancakes.................................. 37

2.   Strawberry Basil Honey Ricotta Toast 38

3.   Overnight Pomegranate Muesli 38

4.   Breakfast Pizza 39

5.   Power Peach Smoothie Bowl 40

6.   Spinach, Sun-Dried Tomato, and Feta Egg Wraps 40

7.   Toasts with Avocado Cream Cheese... 41

8.   Omelette with Spinach and Cheese 42

9.   Bruschetta with Tomato and Basil 43

10.   Chicken Wrap Tortilla Bread and Fried Chicken...................... 43

11.	Vegetable Frittata	44
12.	Strawberry and Lemon Millet Bowl	45
13.	Whipped Feta and Olive Toasts	46
14.	Greek Yogurt Pancakes	46
15.	Baked Eggs with Avocado and Feta	47
16.	Spinach and Egg Breakfast Wraps	48
17.	Almond Banana Pancakes	49
18.	Parmesan Omelet	50
19.	Vanilla Pancakes	50
20.	Quesadillas	51

Grain, Bean & Pasta 53

21.	Pasta with Cashew Sauce	53
22.	Mediterranean-Style Beans and Greens	54
23.	Broccoli and Carrot Pasta Salad	55
24.	Bean and Veggie Pasta	55
25.	Tomato Basil Pasta	56
26.	Bulgur Pilaf with Kale and Tomatoes	57
27.	Cranberry and Almond Quinoa	58
28.	Cumin Quinoa Pilaf	58
29.	Mixed Vegetable Pasta	59
30.	Tuna & Rosemary Pizza	60
31.	Three Bean Mix	61
32.	Mediterranean Pinto Beans	62
33.	Spiced Chickpeas	63
34.	Chili-Garlic Rice with Halloumi	63
35.	Creole Spaghetti	64

36. Classic Spaghetti Aglio E Olio.. 65

37. Pasta and Chickpea Soup 66

38. Lemon Garlic Pasta 67

39. Pesto Pasta.. 68

40. Vegan Carbonara 69

Side & Appetizers 71

41. Spicy Wilted Greens with Garlic 71

42. Roasted Broccolini with Garlic and Romano........................... 71

43. White Beans with Rosemary, Sage, And Garlic 72

44. Moroccan-Style Couscous 73

45. Grilled Broccoli Rabe... 74

46. Grilled Radicchio with Blue Cheese 74

47. Roasted Garlicky Kale.. 75

48. Ginger and Orange Rice 76

49. Couscous with Olives and Feta Cheese.................................... 77

50. Roasted Zucchini 77

51. Italian Fried Calamari 78

52. Roasted Chickpeas 79

53. Baked Beet Chips 80

54. Roasted Pumpkin Seeds 81

55. Beet Hummus.. 81

56. Tuna Salad Sandwiches.. 82

57. Peach Caprese Skewers 83

58. Hummus... 83

59. Eggplant Dip 84

60. Artichoke Crab... 86

Soup & Salad 88

61. Creamy Tomato Hummus Soup 88

62. Mediterranean Tomato Hummus Soup 88

63. Chickpea Soup with Pasta 89

64. Nettle Soup 90

65. Spanish Cold Soup (Ajo Blanco) 91

66. Miso Soup 91

67. Fig and Arugula Salad 92

68. Watermelon Feta Salad 93

69. Citrus Fennel Salad 93

70. Mixed Salad with Balsamic Honey Dressing 95

71. Citrus Salad with Kale and Fennel 97

72. Cucumber and Tomato Salad 98

73. Pear Salad with Roquefort Cheese 99

74. Grilled Eggplant Salad 100

75. Mushroom Salad with Blue Cheese and Arugula 101

76. Artichoke Salad 102

77. Avocado and Cucumber Salad 102

78. Chicken and Broccoli Salad 103

79. Caprese Salad 103

80. Greek Salad with Grilled Chicken 104

Vegetable Main 106

81. Beet and Carrot Fritters with Yogurt Sauce 106

82. Socca Pan Pizza with Herbed Ricotta, Fresh Tomato, And Balsamic Glaze 107

83. Grilled Eggplant Stacks 108

84. Quick Hummus Bowls 109

85. Easy Veggie Wrap 110

86. Italian Eggplant Sandwich... 111

87. Tomato Stuffed with Cheese & Peppers 112

88. Spiralized Carrot with Peas 113

89. Catalan-Style Spinach... 113

90. Simple Sautéed Cauliflower.. 114

91. Feta and Cheese Couscous 115

92. Vegetable Cakes 116

93. Grilled Eggplant with Basil and Parsley... 117

94. Orzo with Herbs 118

95. Basil Artichoke 118

96. Chili Broccoli 119

97. Cauliflower Rice 120

98. Veggie Rice Bowls with Pesto Sauce 121

99. Sautéed Spinach and Leeks 122

100. Simple Honey-Glazed Baby Carrots... 122

Poultry 124

101. Chicken Bruschetta Burgers 124

102. Chicken Gyros with Tzatziki Sauce.. 125

103. Sicilian Olive Chicken... 126

104. Chicken Skillet with Mushrooms 127

105. Grilled Chicken Breasts with Spinach Pesto 128

106. Vegetable & Chicken Skewers 128

107. Tuscan Style Chicken... 129

108. Turkey with Rigatoni... 130

109. Greek Turkey Meatballs.. 131

110. Turkey Patties 132

111. Hot Chicken with Black Beans 133

112. Turkey Pepperoni Pizza 133

113. Bruschetta Chicken Burgers 134

114. Lemony Turkey and Pine Nuts 135

115. Lemon and Paprika Herb-Marinated Chicken 136

116. Mediterranean Chicken Salad Wraps 137

117. Spiced Chicken Thighs with Saffron Basmati 138

118. Chicken Souvlaki 139

119. One-Pot Chicken Pesto Pasta 140

120. Greek Turkey Cutlets 141

Meats 143

121. Sausages with Vegetables 143

122. Kofta Kebabs 143

123. Pork Chops in Wine Sauce 144

124. Grilled Lamb Chops 145

125. Pan-Seared Pork Chops 146

126. Hamburgers 147

127. Greek-Style Lamb Burgers 148

128. Easy Pork Chops in Tomato Sauce 149

129. Fennel Lamb Chops 150

130. Lamb Meatballs with Tzatziki 152

131. Basil Meatballs 153

132. Thyme Pork Steak 153

133. Lamb Chops with Herb Butter 154

134. Beef & Eggplant Casserole 155

135. Crusted Herb Pork Chops 156

136. Spicy Lamb Burgers with Harissa Mayo 157

137. Greek-Style Ground Beef Pita Sandwiches 158

138. Pork Souvlaki Pita 159

139. Spiced Lamb and Beef Kebabs 160

140. Sage Pork Chops with Sweet & Spicy Chutney 161

Fish & Seafood 163

141. Pesto Fish Fillet 163

142. Salmon and Mango Mix 163

143. Trout and Tzatziki Sauce 164

144. Lemon-Parsley Swordfish 165

145. Grilled Octopus 166

146. Spaghetti with Tuna and Capers 167

147. Crusty Halibut 168

148. Smokey Glazed Tuna 169

149. Mussels O' Marine 170

150. Hot and Fresh Fishy Steaks 171

151. Garlic & Lemon Sea Bass 172

152. Crispy Garlic Shrimp 173

153. Salmon with Vegetables 174

154. Baked White Fish with Vegetables 175

155. Garlic Scallops 176

156. Dill Chutney Salmon 176

157. Garlic-Butter Parmesan Salmon and Asparagus 177

158. Grilled Lemon Pesto Salmon 178

159. Steamed Trout with Lemon Herb Crust 179

160. Tomato Tuna Melts 180

Snacks 182

161. Mediterranean Chickpea Salad 182

162. Authentic Mediterranean Hummus 184

163. Hummus with Parsley and Pita 185

164. Feta Cheese Cubes with Herbs and Olives 186

165. Fried Spicy Shrimps 187

166. Grilled Sardines on Toast 187

167. Squash and Zucchini Fritters 188

168. Mediterranean Trail Mix 189

169. Seared Halloumi with Pesto and Tomato 190

170. Stuffed Cucumber Cups 190

171. Apple Chips with Chocolate Tahini 191

172. Strawberry Caprese Skewers 192

173. Herbed Labneh Vegetable Parfaits 192

174. Fool-Proof Hummus 193

175. Pea and Avocado Guacamole 194

176. Caprese Skewers 195

177. Mini Quesadillas 195

178. Greek Yogurt Parfait 197

179. Bruschetta 197

180. Smashed Avocado Toast 198

Desserts: 200

181. Strawberries with Balsamic Vinegar 200

182. Frozen Mango Raspberry 200

183. Grilled Stone Fruit with Honey 201

184. Orange Mug Cakes 201

185. Fruit and Nut Chocolate Bark 202

186. Cozy Superfood Hot Chocolate 203

187. Spicy Hot Chocolate... 204

188. Fruit Cups with Orange Juice 205

189. Strawberry & Cocoa Yogurt 205

190. Raspberries & Lime Frozen Yogurt 206

191. Maple Grilled Pineapple 206

192. Yogurt and Berry Tiramisu 207

193. Strawberry and Avocado Medley............................ 208

194. No Bake Mosaic Cake 208

195. Chocolate pudding 209

196. Greek yogurt bowl 210

197. Yogurt Parfait with Granola................................... 210

198. Saffron and Cardamom Ice Cream 211

199. Orange Olive Oil Mug Cakes 212

200. Dark Chocolate Bark with Fruit and Nuts 213

Appendix: Conversions & Equivalents 214

Appendix 2: Recipe Index... 216

Table of Content

88.	Spiralized Carrot with Peas	104
89.	Catalan-Style Spinach	104
90.	Simple Sautéed Cauliflower	105
91.	Feta and Cheese Couscous	106
92.	Vegetable Cakes	107
93.	Grilled Eggplant with Basil and Parsley	108
94.	Orzo with Herbs	109
95.	Basil Artichoke	109
96.	Chili Broccoli	110
97.	Cauliflower Rice	111
98.	Veggie Rice Bowls with Pesto Sauce	112
99.	Sautéed Spinach and Leeks	113
100.	Simple Honey-Glazed Baby Carrots	113

Poultry 115

101.	Chicken Bruschetta Burgers	115
102.	Chicken Gyros with Tzatziki Sauce	116
103.	Sicilian Olive Chicken	117
104.	Chicken Skillet with Mushrooms	118
105.	Grilled Chicken Breasts with Spinach Pesto	119
106.	Vegetable & Chicken Skewers	119
107.	Tuscan Style Chicken	120
108.	Turkey with Rigatoni	121
109.	Greek Turkey Meatballs	122
110.	Turkey Patties	123
111.	Hot Chicken with Black Beans	124
112.	Turkey Pepperoni Pizza	124

113.	Bruschetta Chicken Burgers	125
114.	Lemony Turkey and Pine Nuts	126
115.	Lemon and Paprika Herb-Marinated Chicken	127
116.	Mediterranean Chicken Salad Wraps	128
117.	Spiced Chicken Thighs with Saffron Basmati Rice	129
118.	Chicken Souvlaki	130
119.	One-Pot Chicken Pesto Pasta	131
120.	Greek Turkey Cutlets	132
Meats		134
121.	Sausages with Vegetables	134
122.	Kofta Kebabs	134
123.	Pork Chops in Wine Sauce	135
124.	Grilled Lamb Chops	136
125.	Pan-Seared Pork Chops	137
126.	Hamburgers	138
127.	Greek-Style Lamb Burgers	139
128.	Easy Pork Chops in Tomato Sauce	140
129.	Fennel Lamb Chops	141
130.	Lamb Meatballs with Tzatziki	142
131.	Basil Meatballs	143
132.	Thyme Pork Steak	143
133.	Lamb Chops with Herb Butter	144
134.	Beef & Eggplant Casserole	145
135.	Crusted Herb Pork Chops	146
136.	Spicy Lamb Burgers with Harissa Mayo	147
137.	Greek-Style Ground Beef Pita Sandwiches	148

138.	Pork Souvlaki Pita	149
139.	Spiced Lamb and Beef Kebabs	150
140.	Sage Pork Chops with Sweet & Spicy Chutney	151

Fish & Seafood 153

141.	Pesto Fish Fillet	153
142.	Salmon and Mango Mix	153
143.	Trout and Tzatziki Sauce	154
144.	Lemon-Parsley Swordfish	155
145.	Grilled Octopus	156
146.	Spaghetti with Tuna and Capers	157
147.	Crusty Halibut	158
148.	Smokey Glazed Tuna	159
149.	Mussels O' Marine	160
150.	Hot and Fresh Fishy Steaks	161
151.	Garlic & Lemon Sea Bass	162
152.	Crispy Garlic Shrimp	163
153.	Salmon with Vegetables	164
154.	Baked White Fish with Vegetables	165
155.	Garlic Scallops	166
156.	Dill Chutney Salmon	166
157.	Garlic-Butter Parmesan Salmon and Asparagus	167
158.	Grilled Lemon Pesto Salmon	168
159.	Steamed Trout with Lemon Herb Crust	169
160.	Tomato Tuna Melts	170

Snacks 172

161.	Mediterranean Chickpea Salad	172

162.	Authentic Mediterranean Hummus	173
163.	Hummus with Parsley and Pita	174
164.	Feta Cheese Cubes with Herbs and Olives	175
165.	Fried Spicy Shrimps	176
166.	Grilled Sardines on Toast	176
167.	Squash and Zucchini Fritters	177
168.	Mediterranean Trail Mix	178
169.	Seared Halloumi with Pesto and Tomato	179
170.	Stuffed Cucumber Cups	179
171.	Apple Chips with Chocolate Tahini	180
172.	Strawberry Caprese Skewers	181
173.	Herbed Labneh Vegetable Parfaits	181
174.	Fool-Proof Hummus	182
175.	Pea and Avocado Guacamole	183
176.	Caprese Skewers	184
177.	Mini Quesadillas	184
178.	Greek Yogurt Parfait	186
179.	Bruschetta	186
180.	Smashed Avocado Toast	187
Desserts:		189
181.	Strawberries with Balsamic Vinegar	189
182.	Frozen Mango Raspberry	189
183.	Grilled Stone Fruit with Honey	190
184.	Orange Mug Cakes	190
185.	Fruit and Nut Chocolate Bark	191
186.	Cozy Superfood Hot Chocolate	192

187.	Spicy Hot Chocolate	193
188.	Fruit Cups with Orange Juice	194
189.	Strawberry & Cocoa Yogurt	194
190.	Raspberries & Lime Frozen Yogurt	195
191.	Maple Grilled Pineapple	195
192.	Yogurt and Berry Tiramisu	196
193.	Strawberry and Avocado Medley	197
194.	No Bake Mosaic Cake	197
195.	Chocolate pudding	198
196.	Greek yogurt bowl	199
197.	Yogurt Parfait with Granola	199
198.	Saffron and Cardamom Ice Cream	200
199.	Orange Olive Oil Mug Cakes	201
200.	Dark Chocolate Bark with Fruit and Nuts	202
Appendix: Conversions & Equivalents		203
Appendix 2: Recipe Index		205

Introduction

Regardless of your kitchen experience, there is something fulfilling about fixing a good-quality meal and sharing it with your lover. Cooking is one of the healthiest ways to build relationships because it brings people together. It is also a unique way of encouraging conversation between lovers, that can contribute to their connection. Cooking for two may not seem like much work, but believe me, it's worth the time.

When you and your special someone is looking on adopting a healthier way of eating, Mediterranean diet is the way to go. When you cook and explore it kitchen idea with your loved one, it creates unique moment that builds the needed connection. The Mediterranean diet for two can be discovered via it improved cooking and eating pattern. When you make that decision to embrace the eating lifestyle, it can contribute loads of benefits to your wellbeing.

Studies indicate that, the diet has a significant impact on preventing heart disease, stroke, and risk factors like obesity, diabetes, high cholesterol, and high blood pressure. Some research suggests that a Mediterranean diet high in olive oil may aid in the body's removal of extra cholesterol from the arteries and maintenance of open blood vessels.

Beyond physical health, the Mediterranean diet also enhances mental well-being. Foods rich in antioxidants and amino acids help cleanse your cells of toxins primarily left by animal proteins, which are detrimental to your health. Amino acids are important for brain cell development and maintaining healthy cognitive functions.

Another important reason you can go for Mediterranean diet is because of the values of it delicious meals. The Mediterranean diet cookbook for two is intended to inspire you to spend less but quality time learning new, scrumptious, and healthy recipes. In fact, you might be new to cooking, the Mediterranean diet is the perfect diet for your healthier lifestyle.

All good cuisine you may find is delicious, but the conventional Mediterranean diet is unique of all. Due to their freshness, lightness, speed, and simplicity of preparation, you can choose delicious meals that feature healthy ingredients. Consequently, you will discover a few recipes that feature yogurt, seafood, whole grains, legumes, and fruit. They are regulars in the Mediterranean kitchen, and their particular health advantages are reasons for it acceptance.

Additionally, I hope you'll be motivated to collaborate with that special someone to incorporate the other components of the Mediterranean diet. Such component involves you to increase your physical activity, elevate the quality of your meals, and take time to enjoy every moment of the kitchen experience.

Overview of the Mediterranean Diet

You may be wondering what exactly is the Mediterranean diet, and you need to be aware that it's more of a lifestyle than a normal diet. The Mediterranean diet is a healthy eating pattern that originates from Mediterranean countries such as Greece, Italy, Spain, France, and northern Africa. It drew on the coastal eating styles of Greece, Italy, and Spain but it has since incorporated elements from other Mediterranean dishes such as those in the Levant and North Africa.

It's a way of eating that will help you to live a happy, full life with your partner. It can help you lose some pounds and strengthen your heart while providing yourself with all of the nutrients you need for a long, healthy life. Those that follow this diet often are at a lower risk of cancer, Alzheimer's, enjoy an extended lifespan and overall better cardiovascular health. The Mediterranean diet consists of foods that are rich in healthy oils, filled with vegetable and fruit, and foods that are low in saturated fat.

The Mediterranean diet is a heart healthy eating plan that's based on the food that can be found in the Mediterranean, which includes quite a number of countries. It includes pasta, rice, vegetables and fruit, but it does not allow for much red meat. Nuts are also a part of this diet, but they should be limited due to the fact that they are high in fat and calories.

Also, the diet limits your fat consumption and discourages the eating of saturated or trans-fat. Both types have been linked to heart disease. Grains are often served whole and bread is an important part of the lifestyle, but butter doesn't really play a roll. Wine, however, has a huge place in the Mediterranean diet both in cooking and including a glass with each meal if you are of age. The primary source of fat in this diet are olive oil and fatty fish including herring, mackerel, albacore, tuna, sardines, salmon and trout, which are rich in omega-3 fatty acids.

With the Mediterranean diet, you are giving your body the nutrients and vitamins it needs, so you won't feel hungry. However, it requires a large commitment to eating natural foods, removing temptation, and cooking regular meals. If you love to cook this isn't much of a change, but for those that have few skills in the kitchen it can be a daunting, but well rewarding task. Of course, like with any diet stay well hydrated, and moderate exercise will go a long way!

The History of the Mediterranean Diet

The Mediterranean diet is a dietary pattern that has been associated with a lower risk of various chronic diseases and improved overall health outcomes. The history of the Mediterranean diet dates back to ancient times, when people living in the Mediterranean basin, particularly in Greece and Italy, consumed a diet based on plant-based foods, such as fruits, vegetables, whole grains, nuts, and legumes, along with moderate amounts of fish and seafood, and smaller amounts of dairy, poultry, and red meat.

The concept of the Mediterranean diet was first introduced in the 1950s by the American physiologist Ancel Keys, who conducted the Seven Countries Study, a landmark study that examined the dietary patterns and health outcomes of populations in different countries. Keys observed that people living in the Mediterranean region had a lower risk of heart disease compared to those in other regions, and he attributed this to their traditional diet.

Since then, numerous studies have been conducted to investigate the health benefits of the Mediterranean diet. In 1993, the Mediterranean Diet Pyramid was developed by the Old ways Preservation Trust in collaboration with the Harvard School of Public Health and the World Health Organization, which highlighted the key components of the Mediterranean diet and provided practical guidelines for adopting the diet.

Today, the Mediterranean diet is widely recognized as one of the healthiest dietary patterns in the world and is recommended by many health organizations, including the American Heart Association and the World Health Organization, as a way to promote overall health and prevent chronic diseases such as heart disease, diabetes, and cancer.

The Key Components of the Mediterranean Diet

The key components include:

Lots of fruits and vegetables: The Mediterranean diet emphasizes the consumption of a variety of colorful fruits and vegetables, as they are rich in vitamins, minerals, and fiber.

Whole grains: The diet includes whole grains such as brown rice, quinoa, and whole wheat bread, which are high in fiber and provide sustained energy.

Legumes: Legumes such as beans, chickpeas, and lentils are a good source of plant-based protein and fiber and are often eaten in Mediterranean dishes.

Healthy fats: The diet includes healthy fats such as olive oil, nuts, and seeds. These foods are rich in monounsaturated and polyunsaturated fats, which can help lower cholesterol levels and reduce the risk of heart disease.

Fish and seafood: The Mediterranean diet includes fish and seafood as a primary source of protein. Fish such as salmon, tuna, and sardines are high in omega-3 fatty acids, which can help reduce inflammation in the body.

Moderate dairy consumption: The diet includes moderate consumption of dairy products, such as cheese and yoghurt. These foods are a good source of calcium and other essential nutrients.

Red meat in moderation: The diet includes moderate consumption of red meat, such as beef and lamb, but it is not the main source of protein.

Herbs and spices: The Mediterranean diet relies on herbs and spices to add flavor to dishes instead of using salt or other flavorings.

The Mediterranean Diet Food Pyramid

The Mediterranean diet food pyramid was designed by the Harvard School of Public Health, the World Health Organization, and Old Ways Preservation Trust, a food and nutrition nonprofit. It's a visual guideline that makes the principles of the diet easy to understand and follow.

Vegetables, fruits, whole grains, olive oil, legumes, nuts, seeds, herbs, and spices make up the base or the widest part of the pyramid, because these are foods to eat at every meal.

Seafood, especially oily fish, occupies the next level and should be eaten often, or at least twice each week. Poultry, eggs, cheese, and yogurt follow, with a guideline of eating moderate portions daily to weekly.

The smallest part of the pyramid represents meat and sweets, which should be enjoyed less often and reserved for special occasions. Water is the beverage of choice. However, if you enjoy red wine, it does have some heart health benefits when consumed in moderation—although it may not be appropriate for everyone.

Health Benefits of the Mediterranean Diet

The Mediterranean diet lifestyle is one of the healthiest diet in the world. In fact, it is one of the most researched and extensively acclaimed diets, as proven by substantial amount of scientific studies conducted over the past sixty years. The following are some of the amazing health benefits offered by this way of eating.

Long and Healthy Life: The Mediterranean cuisine is often referred to as the healthiest cuisine in the world, and the diet doesn't stray too far away. Because it is based mostly on fresh vegetables and fruits, healthy oils and whole grains, as well as lean meat and seafood, it's not hard to see why this diet is considered to be healthy. Mix with a glass of red wine, and you've got yourself a fun, easy-going diet.

Strong Bones: The high level of healthy fats and olive oil provides nutrients that can help with bone density. In a research printed in the JAMA Internal Medicine journal, scientists studied 90,000 women with an average age of 64. The women had fewer occurrences of bone breakage and a lower rate of osteoporosis.

Healthy Heart: Scientific evidence easily connects good heart health with certain foods, mainly vegetables, fruits, olive oil, and nuts. The Mediterranean diet has it all! The Mediterranean diet is all about highlighting healthy fats. Instead of using the usual cooking oil, the diet uses olive oil, which contains healthy fat that is good for the heart. With that said, the Mediterranean Diet can help decrease your risk of heart failure.

Weight Loss: Although the main focus of this diet is not weight loss, it will surely help with it if that's what you're looking for. Here is the point of view: fresh, clean food combined with whole grains, good fats, less sugar and plenty of liquids coupled with copious amounts of exercise. By transitioning to healthy foods and a healthy lifestyle, you'll shed pounds without causing drastic imbalances in your body. Also, it is known that plant-based diets like the Mediterranean diet help lose weight. The mere fact that you stopped eating junk food and processed food with sugar and unhealthy fats is already a perfect start to weight loss!

High Blood Pressure: The healthy fats found in the Mediterranean Diet are probably one of the keys to the lower blood pressure rates found in people following this eating pattern. These healthier fats include the monounsaturated fats found in olive oil and some nuts and the omega-3 fats found in most fish.

Controls Diabetes: Because it focuses on fresh Ingredients: and it packs plenty of vitamins, antioxidants, and minerals, this diet is an ideal way of controlling diabetes. This lifestyle controls excess insulin, which in turn lowers our blood sugar levels. Regulating blood sugar levels is vastly vital to living a healthier lifestyle.

There is a need for balancing a lot of whole foods into this plan to find quality sources of protein and consume carbs that are low in sugar. That makes the body burn fat much more efficiently, and you will have more energy as a result. In short, a natural diet with fresh produce is a natural combater of diabetes.

Affordable: The Mediterranean diet is accessible even if you're on a budget. Legumes, vegetables, fruits, herbs, whole grains, and olive oil are not as expensive as they sound, but they offer so much versatility in the kitchen.

Cancer: There is a strong consensus among health care professionals that following the Mediterranean Diet is linked to reduced overall cancer rates. Cancer-lowering associations are even stronger for digestive tract cancers, as reported in a 2017 study in Cancer Genomics and Proteomics.

Boost Brain Power: The Mediterranean Diet can also counteract the brain's reduced ability to perform. Choosing this lifestyle will help you preserve your memory, leading to an overall increase in your cognitive health.

Encourage Relaxation: The Mediterranean Diet surprisingly enough, can encourage relaxation. The diet can lower your levels of insulin and make you feel at ease. High blood sugar can cause you to be hyperactive and later crash; but eating balanced meals with lots of whole grains, fruits, veggies, etc. actually helps stabilize blood sugar, allowing you to relax and rest. Since a significant component of this lifestyle is eating with the family at the dinner table, relaxation is maximized. With a home-cooked meal in your comfort zone, relaxation will be evident with this diet.

Enhance Your Mood: The diet can help you to be positive, even when things aren't going your way. Healthy living does that. When you have eaten enough food to fuel you with lots of nutrients, your body notices. Fulfillment and productivity enhance your mood. For one, applying the diet correctly will make you feel like you're doing something good for yourself, and thus improves your overall mood.

Improve Skin Condition: Fish have Omega-3 fatty acids. They strengthen the skin membrane and make it more elastic and firmer. Olive oil, red wine, and tomatoes contain a lot of antioxidants to protect against skin damage brought about by chemical reactions and prolonged sun exposure.

Alzheimer's Disease: As we age, our brains shrink. In several studies, including one published in Neurology in 2017, researchers found that people who eat according to the Mediterranean Diet generally maintain a bigger brain size than those who don't eat this way. Some doctors speculate that having a larger brain may help lower the risk of brain diseases, including dementia and Alzheimer's.

Cardiovascular Disease: Most health care professionals agree that the Mediterranean Diet lowers the risk of heart disease, an association mentioned in Dietary Guidelines for Americans.

Tip and Tricks for Mediterranean Diet

The Mediterranean Diet is a lifestyle choice that has many health benefits, and it is easy to maintain as well. First, you must know what foods are allowed on the Mediterranean diet. On a typical day of eating on the Mediterranean Diet, your plate would be filled with fruits and vegetables firstly, then an appropriate amount of meat or fish, followed by starchy carbs like whole-grain rice or pasta. Alongside these three food groups, there will also be plenty of olive oil-based dressings and sauces used liberally throughout meals. This gives you an idea about how varied your options can be when following this way of life. While many people dive right into this new way of eating without planning or understanding the ins and outs of what they should be doing to achieve their goals, there are some tricks you can use to make your journey easier. That is precisely what this chapter is going to be about | it will discuss some tricks for ensuring your success in adapting to the Mediterranean diet.

How to Start

The Mediterranean lifestyle is an easy way to get back on track with your healthy eating habits. It has been found that people who live in this region have lower obesity, heart disease, and diabetes rates than the average person. The Mediterranean diet is an excellent choice for anyone looking to get healthier, lower cholesterol levels, and lose weight.

Now that you have been introduced to the wonders of a Mediterranean diet, it is time to show you how easy and delicious transitioning into this lifestyle can be. The following are five-step guide to making the transition from your old ways with healthy eating habits, so come with me on an exciting journey to better health.

Use Olive Oil: It is necessary to substitute other fats with olive oil if you want the benefits of the Mediterranean diet. Olive oil is central to this type of diet, and it contains good fats. But, if you do not replace other types of fat with olive oil, you will not get those benefits.

Eat Vegetables as the Main Dish: One of the main features that set the Mediterranean Diet apart from most other diets is its high consumption of vegetables. Greeks consume almost a pound per day, which can be seen in their cooking techniques, such as sautéed green beans with olive oil or tomato sauce.

Cook Simple Mediterranean Meals: The Mediterranean diet is a refreshing change from the Western standard. It consists of real food that can make your life happier and healthier, like omelets with fresh vegetables or grilled fish topped with tomatoes. You might not have to cook from scratch every day, but learning 2-3 essential dishes will help you in the long run.

Try Going Vegan One Day: A Week It may have been that the Greeks' diet was so healthy because they abstained from animal products for roughly half of their year. This would make sense as a religious practice and potentially an important factor in why this population had much better health than others due to less meat consumption and more plant-based foods.

Do Not Add Meat to Everything: Many people see vegetables on the recommendation list, but what does meat add to a diet? Studies show that reducing your red and white meats intake will have better health benefits. Try these guidelines:

one serving of lean beef once per week | three servings of chicken weekly, one every two days, with fish as an alternative for those who do not like seafood.

Cooking Tips for Two

Cooking for two is an intimate experience that brings people closer to the heart of Mediterranean cuisine. Taking up the Mediterranean diet together presents a special chance for bonding around shared interest in food, travel, and wellness. Let's begin this adventure together by appreciating how much fresh produce is readily available in your local markets. Plan your meals a group, making sure to include arrange of vibrant fruits, veg tables, nutritious grains, and lean proteins in your menu.

Cooking together may be a fun pastime. Try out some classic Mediterranean recipes and learn about the various cuisines that comprise this diet. Use a lot of olive oil when you cook and enjoy the unique flavors it ad s. Share meals with one another to embrace the social side of eating and develop a stronger bond and respect for another's presence. Here are some practical tips and guidelines to help you create Mediterranean meals for two:

Portioning ingredients: Adapting recipes for two people requires careful consideration of ingredient quantities. Consider proportions when choosing ingredients to ensure the perfect balance of dishes.

Freshness is key: The essence of Mediterranean cuisine is using fresh, high-quality ingredients. Choose seasonal produce, herbs, and spices to enhance the flavors of your dishes.

Modular recipes: Give preference to recipes that can be customized. For example, you can prepare a basic recipe and add different proteins, vegetables, or seasonings according to your preferences.

Batch cooking and freezing: Consider batch cooking ingredients, such as grains, sauces, or roasted vegetables. Freeze portions for future meals, and then weekday cooking will become easy.

Balanced meals: The Mediterranean diet emphasizes a balance of protein, healthy fats, whole grains, flavorful herbs and seasonings, fruits, and vegetables. Create complete meals that include all these elements.

Mix and match dishes: Experiment with mixing and matching different foods to create unique Mediterranean-style meals. Combine salads, sauces, and main dishes to diversify and make a satisfying menu.

Reasonable portions: To avoid overspending and ensure a balanced diet, practice portion control. Watch your portions to avoid overeating and enjoy your meals.

Share the experience: Cooking for two is not only a meal but also an experience. Share the process of preparing, cooking, and eating with your partner or loved one to create lasting memories.

Celebrate diversity: Mediterranean cuisine is a combination of flavors from different regions. Try dishes from Southern Europe, North Africa, and West Asia to bring variety to your meals.

Get creative with leftovers: Turn leftovers into new creations. Turn last night's main course into a flavorful salad or wrap for a quick and hearty lunch.

Enjoy the experience: Cooking together provides a great opportunity to socialize, experiment, and appreciate the joy of creating together.

Food to Eat and Avoid

Foods to focus on

Beans, legumes, and whole grains: Lentils, cannellini beans, pinto beans, black beans, and chickpeas (garbanzo beans) are used often in Mediterranean meals. They are rich in protein, fiber, and energy-producing B vitamins. Eating more beans and legumes, along with whole grains, is associated with lower disease risk.

Nuts and seeds: While nuts and seeds contain some protein, they are mainly composed of monounsaturated and polyunsaturated fats—the healthy fats that can decrease disease risk. Whole nuts and seeds also contain fiber, protein, and phytonutrients.

Herbs and spices: Along with providing powerful phytonutrients, many herbs and spices contribute to the unique flavor profiles found in Mediterranean cooking. Adding different spices and herbs increases the nutrition, color, and fresh flavors in your meals.

Vegetables and fruits: Plant foods make up the bulk of the diet and form the largest part of the pyramid. Plants contain special components called phytonutrients that ward off diseases and insects. When we eat the plants, those phytonutrients can help us ward off diseases as well. Fiber-rich fruits and veggies can decrease the risk of chronic diseases and bulk up our meals, so we feel full and satisfied.

Poultry, eggs, cheese, and yogurt: As we get closer to the tip of the pyramid, you'll find foods that are eaten often but in smaller amounts. Poultry is consumed in smaller portions than seafood but more often than red meat. Eggs are an inexpensive complete protein source and one of the few natural sources of immune-strengthening vitamin D and brain-boosting choline. Other regular protein staples include yogurt and cheese, which contain calcium and potassium—crucial for bone health—along with probiotics, which help strengthen the immune system.

Olives and olive oil: Following the Mediterranean Diet means eating olives and or olive oil daily. Olives are rich in heart-healthy monounsaturated fatty acids and antioxidants. Additionally, the olive fruit (yes, it's a fruit) contains healthy amounts of fiber and iron.

Oily fish and seafood: Eating seafood two to three times per week reduces the risk of death from any health-related cause, according to a 2006 study in the Journal of the American Medical Association. It's essential during pregnancy and helps children develop a healthy brain and eyes, as outlined in a 2007 study in The Lancet. It has as well been associated with improved memory in adults who are older according to a 2012 study in Neurology. The essential omega-3 fats in fish are found in only a few other foods.

Foods to enjoy in moderation

At the tip of the pyramid, you'll see the words "less often" next to meats and sweets, which means they are eaten only occasionally.

Wine: Wine is an integral part of the Mediterranean Diet and should be sipped slowly to enhance the taste and enjoyment of food. According to the current edition of Dietary Guidelines for Americans, moderate drinking is defined as taking two 5-oz wine glasses each day for males and one glass for females. These amounts appear to have the most health benefits with the least risks.

Sweets: Cakes, cookies, ice cream, candies, and pastries are reserved for holidays and celebrations in the Mediterranean Diet. We suggest a gradual approach in cutting back on sweets. Start with fruit for dessert twice a week while reducing portion sizes of baked goods.

Red meat: Red meat provides essential nutrients, including iron, vitamin B12, and protein, but eating other protein sources such as fish, beans, or nuts often or in place of red meat can lower your risk for several diseases and premature death, according to a 2012 study in the Archives of Internal Medicine. So, eat red meat in smaller amounts, rather like a side dish.

Foods to cut down

Added sugars: These do not include sugars that occur naturally in fruits, vegetables, and dairy foods, but rather sugars added to a product. They are lurking everywhere these days—in condiments, yogurts, bread, and drinks—and you may not realize how much you are consuming. Look for "added sugars" on food labels.

Refined grains: Refined grains are stripped of the bran and germ during milling, and as a result, the majority of available dietary fiber, iron, B vitamins, and phytonutrients are also removed. They're often found in granola bars, bread, desserts, some cereals, and sweet or savory snacks. They're listed on food labels as wheat flour, rice flour, and any flour or grain without the word "whole" in front of it (except oats, which are always a whole grain).

Processed meats: Our big beef with processed meats like deli meats, salami, sausage, and bacon is the amount of salt and fillers in them. Cured meats like prosciutto are preferred but are eaten in small amounts and not every day.

Empty-calorie beverages: Sports drinks, energy drinks, sweetened iced teas, and sodas add only calories and sugar to your diet. Bottom line: Drink water.

Sodium: The majority of the sodium in our diets doesn't come from the salt shaker, but rather, from processed foods like frozen dinners, frozen pizzas, fast food, processed meats, and condiments. Look for no-salt-added or lower-sodium labels on canned foods when buying things like tomatoes, beans, and broth. As for table salt, we use kosher or sea salt in our recipes because the granules are bigger, so you use less per recipe, but a little salt is important when cooking to make the other flavors in your recipe shine.

Breakfast

1. Orange Cardamom Buckwheat Pancakes

Time: 10 minutes | Serves 2

Ingredients:

- ½ cup buckwheat flour
- ½ teaspoon cardamom
- ½ teaspoon baking powder
- ¼ teaspoon baking soda
- ½ cup milk
- ¼ cup plain Greek yogurt
- 1 egg
- ½ teaspoon orange extract
- 1 tablespoon maple syrup (optional)

Method:

1. In a medium bowl, combine the buckwheat flour, cardamom, baking powder, and baking soda.
2. In another bowl, combine the milk, yogurt, egg, orange extract, and maple syrup (if using) and whisk well to combine.
3. Add the wet ingredients to the dry ingredients and stir until the batter is smooth.
4. Heat a nonstick skillet or a griddle over high heat. When the pan is hot, reduce the heat to medium.
5. Pour the batter into the pan to make four 6-inch pancakes. Depending on the size of your pan, you may need to do this in four batches.

Per Serving:

Calories: 196; fat: 6g; carbs: 27g; Protein: 10g

2. Strawberry Basil Honey Ricotta Toast

e: 10 minutes | Serves 2

Ingredients:

d
e milk or low-fat)
t
iced
iced into thin shreds

Method:

1. Toast the bread.
2. In a small bowl, combine the ricotta, honey, and a pinch or two of sea salt. Taste and add additional honey or salt if desired.
3. Spread the mixture evenly over each slice of bread (about 2 tablespoons per slice).
4. Top each piece with sliced strawberries and a few pieces of shredded basil.

Per Serving:

Calories: 275; fat: 8g; carbs: 41g; Protein: 15g

3. Overnight Pomegranate Muesli

Time: 10 minutes | Serves 2

Ingredients:

- ½ cup gluten-free old-fashioned oats
- ¼ cup shelled pistachios
- 3 tablespoons pumpkin seeds
- 2 tablespoons chia seeds
- ¾ cup milk
- ½ cup plain Greek yogurt
- 2 to 3 teaspoons maple syrup (optional)

- ½ cup pomegranate arils

1. In a medium bowl, mix together the oats, pistachios, pumpkin seeds, chia seeds, milk, yogurt, and maple syrup, if using.
2. Divide the mixture between two 12-ounce mason jars or another type of container with a lid. 3.Top each with ¼ cup of pomegranate arils.
3. Cover each jar or container and store in the refrigerator overnight or up to 4 days.
4. Serve cold, with additional milk if desired.

Per Serving:

Calories: 502; fat: 24g; carbs: 60g; Protein: 17g

4. Breakfast Pizza

Time: 15 minutes | Serves 2

Ingredients:

- 2 (6- to 8-inch-long) pieces of whole-wheat naan bread
- 2 tablespoons prepared pesto
- 1 medium tomato, sliced
- 2 large eggs

Method:

1. Heat a large nonstick skillet over medium-high heat. Place the naan bread in the skillet and let it warm for about 2 minutes on each side. The bread should be softened and just starting to turn golden.
2. Spread 1 tablespoon of the pesto on one side of each slice. Top the pesto with tomato slices to cover. Remove the pizzas from the pan and place each one on its own plate.
3. Crack the eggs into the pan, keeping them separated, and cook until the whites are no longer translucent and the yolk is cooked to desired doneness.
4. With a spatula, spoon one egg onto each pizza.

Per Serving:

Calories: 427; fat: 17g; carbs: 10g; Protein: 17g

5. Power Peach Smoothie Bowl

Time: 15 minutes | Serves 2

Ingredients:

- 2 cups packed partially thawed frozen peaches
- ½ cup plain or vanilla Greek yogurt
- ½ ripe avocado
- 2 tablespoons flax meal
- 1 teaspoon vanilla extract
- 1 teaspoon orange extract
- 1 tablespoon honey (optional)

Method:

1. Combine all of the ingredients in a blender and blend until smooth.
2. Pour the mixture into two bowls, and, if desired, sprinkle with additional toppings.

Per Serving:

Calories: 213; fat: 13g; carbs: 23g; Protein: 6g

6. Spinach, Sun-Dried Tomato, and Feta Egg Wraps

Time: 7 minutes | Serves 2

Ingredients:

- 1 tablespoon olive oil
- ¼ cup minced onion
- 3 to 4 tablespoons minced sun-dried tomatoes in olive oil and herbs

- 3 large eggs, beaten
- 1½ cups packed baby spinach
- 1 ounce crumbled feta cheese
- Salt
- 2 (8-inch) whole-wheat tortillas

Method:

1. In a large skillet, heat the olive oil over medium-high heat. Add the onion and tomatoes and sauté for about 3 minutes.
2. Turn the heat down to medium. Add the beaten eggs and stir to scramble them.
3. Add the spinach and stir to combine. Sprinkle the feta cheese over the eggs. Add salt to taste.
4. Warm the tortillas in the microwave for about 20 seconds each.
5. Fill each tortilla with half of the egg mixture. Fold in half or roll them up and serve.

Per Serving:

Calories: 435; fat: 28g; carbs: 31g; Protein: 17g

7. Toasts with Avocado Cream Cheese

Time: 15 minutes | Serves 2

Ingredients:

- 2 slices of whole-grain bread
- 1 ripe avocado
- 4 oz cream cheese, softened
- 1 tablespoon lemon juice
- Salt and pepper to taste
- 1 teaspoon chia seeds (optional for garnish)
- Fresh herbs (such as dill or parsley), chopped (for garnish)

Method:

1. Toast the bread slices to your preferred crispiness.
2. In a bowl, mash the avocado and mix it with the cream cheese and lemon juice until smooth. Season with salt and pepper to taste.
3. Spread the avocado cream cheese mixture evenly on the toasted bread.
4. Garnish with chia seeds and fresh herbs if desired. Serve immediately.

Per Serving:

Calories: 350, Fat: 24g, Carbs: 27g, Protein: 9g

8. Omelette with Spinach and Cheese

Time: 15 minutes | Serves 2

Ingredients:

- 4 large eggs
- 1 cup fresh spinach, chopped
- 1/2 cup shredded cheese (your choice of feta, mozzarella, or cheddar)
- 2 tablespoons olive oil
- Salt and pepper to taste

Method:

- Beat the eggs in a bowl and season with salt and pepper.
- Heat olive oil in a skillet over medium heat. Add spinach and saute until wilted.
- Pour the beaten eggs over the spinach. Cook until the edges start to firm up.
- Sprinkle cheese evenly over the top. Fold the omelet in half and cook until the cheese melts.
- Serve immediately.

Per Serving:

Calories: 300, Fat: 22g, Carbs: 2g, Protein: 20g

9. Bruschetta with Tomato and Basil

Time: 15 minutes | Serves 2

Ingredients:

- 4 slices of rustic bread
- 2 ripe tomatoes, diced
- 1 clove garlic, minced
- 6 fresh basil leaves, chopped
- 2 tablespoons extra virgin olive oil
- Salt and pepper to taste
- Balsamic glaze (optional)

Method:

1. Preheat your grill or broiler. Lightly toast the bread until golden.
2. Combine diced tomatoes, minced garlic, chopped basil, olive oil, salt, and pepper in a bowl.
3. Spoon the tomato mixture evenly over the toasted bread.
4. Drizzle with balsamic glaze if desired.
5. Serve immediately for the best taste.

Per Serving:

Calories: 200, Fat: 9g, Carbs: 27g Protein: 5g

10.   Chicken Wrap Tortilla Bread and Fried Chicken

Time: 15 minutes | Serves 2

Ingredients:

- 2 chicken breasts, thinly sliced
- 1 cup of lettuce, chopped
- 1 shallot, thinly sliced
- 2 tablespoons mustard mayo
- 2 tablespoons spicy ketchup

Method:

1. Season the chicken slices with salt and pepper, then fry until golden brown and cooked through.
2. Warm the tortilla bread slightly in a dry pan for a softer wrap. Spread mustard mayo evenly over each tortilla bread.
3. Lay out the fried chicken, lettuce, and shallots on the tortilla.
4. Drizzle spicy ketchup over the fillings. Carefully roll the tortilla into a wrap, tucking in the edges.
5. Cut the wrap in half and serve immediately.

Per Serving:

Calories: 350, Fat: 15g, Carbs: 33g, Protein: 25g

11.   Vegetable Frittata

Time: 15 minutes | Serves 2

Ingredients:

- 5 large eggs, room temperature
- ¼ cup plain yogurt
- 1 tablespoon olive oil
- ½ leek, trimmed and diced
- ¼ pound asparagus, trimmed and diced
- ½ cup frozen peas
- ½ cup baby spinach
- Salt and pepper, to taste
- 2 ounces' goat cheese, crumbled

Method:

1. In a medium mixing bowl, whisk the eggs with the yogurt. Set aside.
2. Heat the olive oil in a large nonstick frying pan over medium heat. Add the leek, asparagus, peas, and spinach. Season with salt and pepper.

3. Pour the egg mixture on top. Cover and cook on medium-low heat for about 10 minutes.
4. When the frittata is set, flip it. Cook for 2-3 minutes more. Serve the frittata with goat cheese on top.

Per Serving:

Calories 447, fat 30 g, carbs 15 g, Protein 30 g

12.   Strawberry and Lemon Millet Bowl

Time: 15 minutes | Serves 2

Ingredients:

- ½ pound strawberries, hulled and halved
- Juice and zest of 1 lemon
- 1 teaspoon olive oil
- 1 tablespoon honey
- 1 cup whole milk
- ¾ cup millet
- 1 teaspoon pure vanilla extract
- 2 tablespoons walnuts, chopped

Method:

1. Place the milk, lemon juice, and lemon zest in a saucepan.
2. Place the millet and vanilla extract in it.
3. Cook for about 5 minutes, cover with a lid, and remove from heat.
4. Let it steep for 10 minutes. Mix it with a fork, stir in the halved strawberries, honey, and olive oil, and garnish with chopped walnuts.
5. Serve and enjoy.

Per Serving:

Calories 499, fat 14 g, carbs 78 g, Protein 14 g

13.   Whipped Feta and Olive Toasts

Time: 15 minutes | Serves 2

Ingredients:

- 3 ounces' feta cheese
- 2 tablespoons whole milk
- 4 thick slices sourdough bread
- ½ cup kalamata olives, pitted and sliced
- ½ teaspoon dried oregano
- Pinch of freshly ground black pepper

Method:

1. Place the feta cheese and milk in a food processor or blender. Pulse until creamy.
2. Place the sourdough bread slices on a large nonstick skillet over medium heat.
3. Toast for 3 minutes per side or until golden-brown.
4. Spread the whipped feta on each bread slice. Top with the sliced olives.
5. Sprinkle the toasts with dried oregano and a pinch of pepper.

Per Serving:

Calories 346, fat 14 g, carbs 40 g, Protein 14 g

14.   Greek Yogurt Pancakes

e: 15 minutes | Serves 2

Ingredients:

d milk

- 1 large egg
- ½ cup 2% Greek yogurt
- 1 teaspoon vanilla extract
- Maple syrup, for serving
- Fresh fruit, for serving

Method:

1. In a large bowl, mix together the whole wheat flour, all-purpose flour, baking powder, salt, and sugar.
2. In another bowl, combine the almond milk, egg, Greek yogurt, and vanilla extract. Whisk until smooth.
3. Pour the wet ingredients into the dry ingredients and gently stir until just combined. The batter might be slightly lumpy, which is fine; avoid overmixing.
4. Heat a non-stick skillet over medium-high heat and lightly grease it with oil or butter. Pour about 1/4 cup of batter for each pancake onto the hot skillet.
5. Cook for about 2-3 minutes on each side, or until golden brown and cooked through.
6. Serve hot, topped with maple syrup and fresh fruit of your choice.

Per Serving:

Calories: 310; Fat: 5g; Carbs: 52g; Protein: 14g

15.　　Baked Eggs with Avocado and Feta

Time: 15 minutes | Serves 2

Ingredients:

- 1 large avocado
- 4 eggs
- ¼ cup crumbled feta cheese
- Non-stick cooking spray
- Pepper and salt to taste

Method:

1. Preheat the oven to 400°F. Cut the avocado in half and remove the pit. Scoop out a little more avocado to make room for the eggs.
2. Slice each half into 3-4 pieces and set aside.
3. Spray a small oven-safe dish or ramekin with non-stick cooking spray. Place the sliced avocado at the bottom of the dish. Crack an egg into the center of each avocado slice. Season with salt and pepper.
4. Sprinkle the crumbled feta cheese over the eggs.
5. Place the dish in the preheated oven and bake for about 15 minutes, or until the egg whites are set and the yolks are done to your liking.
6. Serve hot, directly from the oven.

Per Serving:

Calories: 280; Fat: 23.5g; Carbs: 9.3g; Protein: 11.3g

16.   Spinach and Egg Breakfast Wraps

Time: 7 minutes | Serves 2

Ingredients:

- 1 tablespoon olive oil
- ¼ cup minced onion
- 3 to 4 tablespoons minced sun-dried tomatoes in olive oil and herbs
- 3 large eggs, whisked
- 1½ cups packed baby spinach
- 1 ounce (28 g) crumbled feta cheese
- Salt, to taste
- 2 (8-inch) whole-wheat tortillas

Method:

1. Heat the olive oil in a large skillet over medium heat. Add the onion and sun-dried tomatoes and sauté for about 3 minutes, or until the onions are softened.
2. Reduce the heat to medium-low. Add the whisked eggs to the skillet and cook, stirring continuously, until they begin to set, about 1-2 minutes. Add the spinach and sprinkle with feta cheese. Season with salt to taste.

3. Cook until the spinach is wilted and the eggs are fully set, about 1-2 more minutes.
4. Remove the skillet from the heat. Warm the tortillas in the microwave for about 20 seconds to make them more pliable.
5. Divide the egg and spinach mixture evenly between the two tortillas. Fold the bottom of each tortilla up over the filling, then fold in the sides and roll up tightly. Cut each wrap in half diagonally and serve immediately.

Per Serving:

Calories: 434; fat: 28g; carbs: 30.8g; protein: 17.2g

17.   Almond Banana Pancakes

Time: 10 minutes | Serves 2

Ingredients:

- ¼ cup almond flour
- ½ teaspoon ground cinnamon
- 3 eggs
- 1 large banana, mashed
- 1 tablespoon almond butter
- 1 teaspoon vanilla extract
- 1 teaspoon olive oil (for cooking)
- Sliced banana, for serving

Method:

1. In a mixing bowl, whisk the eggs until fluffy.
2. Add the mashed banana, vanilla extract, almond butter, cinnamon, and almond flour to the egg mixture. Stir until you have a smooth batter.
3. Heat the olive oil in a skillet over medium heat. Pour spoonfuls of the batter into the skillet to form small pancakes.
4. Cook each pancake for about 2-3 minutes on each side or until golden brown and cooked through.
5. Serve the pancakes hot, topped with additional sliced bananas.

Calories: 306; Carbs: 3.6g; Fat: 26g; Protein: 14.4g

18.   Parmesan Omelet

e: 15 minutes | Serves 2

Ingredients:

ted
- 1 teaspoon coconut oil (for cooking)

Method:

1. In a small bowl, combine the cream cheese, beaten eggs, oregano, and dill until well mixed.
2. Heat the coconut oil in a non-stick frying pan over medium heat. Pour the egg mixture into the heated pan, spreading it evenly.
3. Sprinkle the grated Parmesan cheese over the top of the egg mixture.
4. Cover and cook over low heat for about 10 minutes, or until the eggs are fully set and the bottom is lightly golden.
5. Slide the omelet onto a plate, sprinkle with paprika, and serve immediately.

Per Serving:

s: 148; fat: 11.5g; carbs: 1.4g; protein: 10.6g

19.   Vanilla Pancakes

Time: 15 minutes | Serves 2

Ingredients:

- 6 ounces' plain yogurt
- ½ cup whole-grain flour
- 1 egg, beaten
- 1 teaspoon vanilla extract
- 1 teaspoon baking powder

Method:

1. Heat a non-stick frying pan over medium heat.
2. In a bowl, combine the plain yogurt, whole-grain flour, beaten egg, vanilla extract, and baking powder. Stir until the mixture is smooth.
3. Lightly grease the heated pan with a small amount of oil or butter. Pour the batter into the pan to form pancakes, about 1/4 cup for each pancake.
4. Cook each pancake for about 1 minute on each side or until they are golden brown and cooked through.
5. Serve the pancakes hot with your choice of toppings.

Per Serving:

Calories: 202; Carbs: 29.4g; Fat: 3.8g; Protein: 11.7g

20.   Quesadillas

Time: 10 minutes | Serves 2

Ingredients:

- 1 medium tomato, sliced
- ½ cup fresh basil leaves
- 2 whole-wheat tortillas
- ½ teaspoon ground black pepper
- 1 tablespoon olive oil
- 4 large eggs, scrambled
- ½ cup grated mozzarella cheese, low-fat

Method:

1. In a medium bowl, mix the scrambled eggs with black pepper.
2. Lay out the tortillas on a large plate. Spread the scrambled egg mixture over half of each tortilla.
3. Top the eggs with basil leaves, tomato slices, and mozzarella cheese. Fold the tortillas over the filling to create a half-moon shape.
4. Heat olive oil in a medium pan over medium heat.
5. Once hot, place the quesadillas in the pan and cook for about 2 to 3 minutes per side, or until the tortillas are golden brown and the cheese has melted.
6. Remove the quesadillas from the pan, cut into wedges, and serve immediately.

Per Serving:

Calories: 201; Fat: 10g; Carbs: 15g; Protein: 12.5g

Grain, Bean & Pasta

21.　　Pasta with Cashew Sauce

Time: 15 minutes | Serves 2

Ingredients:

- 2 oz. fresh arugula
- ½ cup peas
- 1½ cups broccoli florets
- 1 small white onion, diced
- 1 Tbsp. extra-virgin olive oil
- Salt and black pepper, to taste
- 4 cherry tomatoes/sun-dried tomatoes, halved
- 4 oz. whole wheat cannelloni pasta

Sauce:

- ½ cup fresh basil
- ½ cup roasted cashews
- 2 garlic cloves
- 2 Tbsp. lemon juice
- ¼ tsp. sea salt
- ½ cup water

Method:

1. Cook pasta following the package directions. Just before the pasta is done, add in the broccoli florets as it finishes cooking.
2. Take out 1 cup of pasta water, drain, and set aside. Meanwhile, prepare your sauce. Combine all the ingredients in the blender until smooth.
3. Heat the oil in a frying pan on medium heat. Add bell peppers, onion, and seasonings and sauté until tender. Stir in sun-dried tomatoes and arugula and cook for 3 minutes.
4. Toss in the pasta with broccoli. Pour the sauce and add some pasta water for desired consistency. Cook for 4 minutes, stirring occasionally.

5. Garnish with grated hard cheese, if desired.

Per Serving:

Calories: 565, Fat: 25 g, Carbs: 73 g, Protein: 19 g

22.   Mediterranean-Style Beans and Greens

Time: 15 minutes | Serves 2

Ingredients:

- 1 can diced tomatoes with juice
- 1 (15-ounce) can cannellini beans, drained and rinsed
- 2 tablespoons chopped green olives, plus 1 or 2 sliced for garnish
- ¼ cup vegetable broth, plus more as needed
- 1 teaspoon extra-virgin olive oil
- 2 cloves garlic, minced
- 4 cups arugula
- ¼ cup freshly squeezed lemon juice

Method:

1. In a medium saucepan, bring the tomatoes, beans and chopped olives to a low boil, adding just enough broth to make the ingredients saucy.
2. Reduce heat to low and simmer for about 5 minutes.
3. Meanwhile, in a large skillet, heat the olive oil over medium-high heat.
4. When the oil is hot and starts to shimmer, add garlic and sauté just until it starts to turn slightly tan, about 30 seconds. Add the arugula and lemon juice, stirring to coat leaves with the olive oil and juice.
5. Cover and reduce heat to low. Simmer for 3 to 5 minutes. Serve beans over the greens and garnish with olive slices.

Per Serving

Calories: 262, Fat: 5.9g, Carbs: 40.4g, Protein: 13.2g

23.   Broccoli and Carrot Pasta Salad

Time: 10 minutes | Serves 2

Ingredients:

- 8 ounces' whole-wheat pasta
- 2 cups broccoli florets
- 1 cup peeled and shredded carrots
- ¼ cup plain Greek yogurt
- Juice of 1 lemon
- 1 teaspoon red pepper flakes
- Sea salt and freshly ground pepper, to taste

Method:

1. Bring a large pot of lightly salted water to a boil. Add the pasta to the boiling water and cook until al dente.
2. Drain and let rest for a few minutes.
3. When cooled, combine the pasta with the veggies, yogurt, lemon juice, and red pepper flakes in a large bowl, and stir thoroughly to combine.
4. Taste and season to taste with salt and pepper. Serve immediately.

Per Serving

Calories: 428, Fat: 2.9g, Carbs: 84.6g, Protein: 15.9g

24.   Bean and Veggie Pasta

Time: 15 minutes | Serves 2

Ingredients:

- 16 ounces' small whole wheat pasta (such as penne, farfalle, or macaroni)
- 5 cups water
- 1 (15-ounce) can cannellini beans, drained and rinsed
- 1 (14.5-ounce) can diced (with juice) or crushed tomatoes
- 1 yellow onion, chopped

- 1 red or yellow bell pepper, chopped
- 2 tablespoons tomato paste
- 1 tablespoon olive oil
- 3 garlic cloves, minced
- ¼ teaspoon crushed red pepper (optional)
- 1 bunch kale, stemmed and chopped
- 1 cup sliced basil
- ½ cup pitted Kalamata olives, chopped

Method:

1. Add the pasta, water, beans, tomatoes (with juice if using diced), onion, bell pepper, tomato paste, oil, garlic, and crushed red pepper (if desired), to a large stockpot or deep skillet with a lid.
2. Bring to a boil over high heat, stirring often.
3. Reduce the heat to medium-high, add the kale, and cook, continuing to stir often, until the pasta is al dente, about 10 minutes.
4. Remove from the heat and let sit for 5 minutes.
5. Garnish with the basil and olives and serve.

Per Serving

Calories: 565, Fat: 17.7g, Carbs: 85.5g, Protein: 18.0g

25.   Tomato Basil Pasta

ne: 5 minutes | Serves 2

Ingredients:

similar pasta

as needed

lices

lakes

½ teaspoon dried oregano

- 10 to 12 fresh sweet basil leaves
- Freshly ground black pepper, to taste

Method:

1. In your Instant Pot, stir together the pasta, stock, and salt.
2. Scatter the tomatoes on top (do not stir). Secure the lid. Select the Manual mode and set the cooking time for 2 minutes at High Pressure.
3. Once cooking is complete, do a quick pressure release. Carefully open the lid. Stir in the red pepper flakes, oregano, and garlic powder.
4. If there's more than a few tablespoons of liquid in the bottom, select Sauté and cook for 2 to 3 minutes until it evaporates.
5. When ready to serve, chiffonade the basil and stir it in. Taste and season with more salt and pepper, as needed. Serve warm.

Per Serving

Calories: 415, Fat: 2.0g, Carbs: 84.2g, Protein: 15.2g

26. Bulgur Pilaf with Kale and Tomatoes

Time: 10minutes | Serves 2

Ingredients:

- 2 tablespoons olive oil
- 2 cloves garlic, minced
- 1 bunch kale, trimmed and cut into bite-sized pieces
- Juice of 1 lemon
- 2 cups cooked bulgur wheat
- 1-pint cherry tomatoes, halved
- Sea salt and freshly ground pepper, to taste

Method:

1. Heat the olive oil in a large skillet over medium heat.
2. Add the garlic and sauté for 1 minute. Add the kale leaves and stir to coat.
3. Cook for 5 minutes until leaves are cooked through and thoroughly wilted.

4. Add the lemon juice, bulgur and tomatoes.
5. Season with sea salt and freshly ground pepper to taste, then serve.

Per Serving

Calories: 300, Fat: 14.0g, Carbs: 37.8g, Protein: 6.2g

27. Cranberry and Almond Quinoa

ne: 15 minutes | Serves 2

Ingredients:

eds

Method:

1. Combine water and quinoa in the Instant Pot. Secure the lid.
2. Select the Manual mode and set the cooking time for 10 minutes at High Pressure.
3. Once cooking is complete, do a quick pressure release. Carefully open the lid.
4. Add sunflower seeds, almonds, and dried cranberries and gently mix until well combined. Serve hot.

Per Serving

Calories: 445, Fat: 14.8g, Carbs: 64.1g, Protein: 15.1g

28. Cumin Quinoa Pilaf

Time: 10 minutes | Serves 2

Ingredients:

- 2 tablespoons extra virgin olive oil
- 2 cloves garlic, minced
- 3 cups water
- 2 cups quinoa, rinsed
- 2 teaspoons ground cumin
- 2 teaspoons turmeric
- Salt, to taste
- 1 handful parsley, chopped

Method:

1. Press the Sauté button to heat your Instant Pot.
2. Once hot, add the oil and garlic to the pot, stir and cook for 1 minute. Add water, quinoa, cumin, turmeric, and salt, stirring well.
3. Lock the lid. Select the Manual mode and set the cooking time for 1 minute at High Pressure.
4. When the timer beeps, perform a natural pressure release for 10 minutes, then release any remaining pressure. Carefully remove the lid.
5. Fluff the quinoa with a fork. Season with more salt, if needed. Sprinkle parsley on top and serve.

Per Serving

Calories: 384, Fat: 12.3g, Carbs: 57.4g, Protein: 12.8g.

29.   Mixed Vegetable Pasta

Time: 15 minutes | Serves 2

Ingredients:

- 1 lb. thin spaghetti
- ½ cup Olive Oil
- 2 garlic cloves, crushed
- Salt, to taste
- ½ cup chopped fresh parsley
- 6 oz. grape tomatoes, halved

- 2 scallions (green onions), chopped
- ½ teaspoon black pepper
- 3 oz. marinated artichoke hearts, drained
- ¼ cup pitted olives, halved
- ¼ cup crumbled feta cheese
- 5 fresh basil leaves, torn
- Zest of ½ lemon
- Crushed red pepper flakes, optional

Method:

1. Cook the spaghetti pasta as per the packet instructions until al dente. Drain and rinse the spaghetti.
2. Heat oil in a large skillet over medium heat.
3. Add garlic and salt to sauté for 10 seconds.
4. Stir in tomatoes, scallions, and parsley. Cook for 30 seconds. Add the drained pasta and toss well with sauce.
5. Adjust seasoning with black pepper and stir in the remaining Ingredients,
6. Serve warm with basil leaves and feta cheese.

Per Serving:

Calories 483, Fat 19.2 g, Carbs 6.1g, Protein 10.9 g

30.   Tuna & Rosemary Pizza

Time: 15 minutes | Serves 2

Ingredients:

- 1 cup canned tuna, oil-free
- ½ cup mozzarella cheese, shredded
- ¼ cup goat's cheese
- 3 tbsp. olive oil
- 1 tbsp. tomato paste
- ½ tsp dried rosemary
- 14 oz. pizza crust

- 1 cup olives, optional

Method:

1. Grease the bottom of a baking dish with one tablespoon of olive oil. Line some parchment paper.
2. Flour the working surface and roll out the pizza dough to the approximate size of your instant pot.
3. Gently fit the dough in the previously prepared baking dish. In a bowl, combine olive oil, tomato paste and rosemary.
4. Whisk together and Spread the mixture over the crust. Sprinkle with goat cheese, mozzarella, and tuna.
5. Place a trivet inside the pot and pour in 1 cup of water. Seal the lid, and cook for 15 minutes on High Pressure.
6. Do a quick release. Remove the pizza from the pot. Cut and serve.

Per Serving:

Calories 532, Fat 16.2 g, Carbs 9.1g, Protein 43.4 g

31.   Three Bean Mix

Time: 12 minutes | Serves 2

Ingredients:

- 1 (4 oz.) can cannellini (white kidney) beans, rinsed and drained
- 1 (4 oz.) can red kidney beans, rinsed and drained
- 1 (4 oz.) can garbanzo beans, rinsed and drained
- 1 cloves garlic, minced
- 2 tablespoons minced fresh parsley, or to taste
- ¼ cup olive oil
- ½ onion, minced
- ½ cup cherry tomatoes, halved
- ¼ cup radish, diced
- 1 avocado diced
- 1 lemon, juiced

- Salt and ground black pepper to taste

Method:

1. Heat oil in a skillet.
2. Add onion, cherry tomatoes and garlic to sauté for 2 minutes.
3. Stir in all the remaining Ingredients.
4. Cook for 5 minutes with occasional stirring
5. Mix well and serve.

Per Serving:

Calories 539, Fat 21 g, Carbs 46.8g, Protein 49.6 g

32.   Mediterranean Pinto Beans

Time: 5 minutes | Serves 2

Ingredients:

- 1 large ripe tomato, seeds and excess pulp removed, diced
- 2 tablespoons finely minced onion
- 4 medium cloves garlic, pressed
- 1 tablespoon balsamic vinegar
- 2 tablespoons extra virgin olive oil
- 4 tablespoons chopped fresh parsley
- Pinch red chili flakes
- Salt and cracked black pepper to taste
- 2 cups (BPA free) pinto beans, drained and rinsed

Method:

1. Add the Ingredients: to a bowl except for the beans.
2. Mix well and let it rest for 5 minutes. Drain and rinse the beans.
3. Toss the beans with the prepared mixture.
4. Let it marinate for 30 minutes. Serve.

Per Serving:

Calories 301, Fat 12.2 g, Carbs 15g, Protein 28.8 g

33.   Spiced Chickpeas

Time: 15 minutes | Serves 2

Ingredients:

- ½ teaspoon Cardamom
- 1 teaspoon Cumin
- 1½ teaspoon Allspice
- ½ teaspoon red pepper flakes to taste
- ½ teaspoon Salt
- 1 cup Cooked chickpeas
- 2 tablespoons Olive oil

Method:

1. In a bowl, combine the spices and salt.
2. Add the chickpeas to the spice mixture.
3. Over medium heat, warm the olive oil in a pan.
4. Add the chickpea mixture, occasionally stirring.
5. Remove skillet from heat and serve with yogurt.

Per Serving:

Calories 642, Fat 14.7 g, Carbs 11.5g, Protein 43 g

34.   Chili-Garlic Rice with Halloumi

Time: 10 minutes | Serves 2

Ingredients:

- 1 cup water
- 1 tbsp. brown sugar
- 1 tbsp. rice vinegar

- 1 tbsp. sweet chili sauce
- 1 tbsp. olive oil
- 1 tsp fresh minced garlic
- 6 ounces Halloumi cheese, cubed
- ½ cup rice
- ¼ cup chopped fresh chives, for garnish

Method:

1. Heat the oil on Sauté and fry the halloumi for 5 minutes until golden brown. Set aside.
2. To the pot, add water, garlic, olive oil, vinegar, sugar, soy sauce, and chili sauce and mix well until smooth. Stir in rice noodles.
3. Seal the lid and cook on High Pressure for 3 minutes. Release the Pressure quickly. Split the rice between bowls.
4. Top with fried halloumi and sprinkle with fresh chives before serving.

Per Serving:

Calories 533, Fat 10.3 g, Carbs 8.6g, Protein 16 g

35.   Creole Spaghetti

Time: 15 minutes | Serves 2

Ingredients:

- 1 extra virgin olive oil
- 1¼ lbs. ground beef (85% lean)
- ¼ lb. country ham, cut into ¼" pieces (about ¾ cup)
- 1 can tomato sauce
- ½ cup sofrito
- ½ Tbsp. minced garlic
- ½ Tbsp. sugar
- ¼ tsp ground cumin
- ¼ tsp oregano
- ¼ packet sazon with coriander & annatto

- ¼ cup manzanillo olives stuffed with minced pimientos, chopped
- ½ cup finely chopped fresh cilantro, divided
- ½ tsp. adobo all-purpose seasoning with pepper
- ½ lb. spaghetti
- Parmesan cheese, to taste

Method:

1. Add the beef to a pan with hot olive oil over medium-high heat. Cook for approximately 6 minutes, or until browned. Transfer the beef over to the plate.
2. Put the ham back in the pan and reheat it over medium heat. Cook for approximately 4 minutes, stirring periodically, or until the ham is golden brown.
3. To the pan, add the tomato sauce, garlic, sugar, cumin, oregano, and sazon. Simmer the tomato sauce mixture until it begins to boil.
4. Add the Adobo, 1/8 cup coriander, olives, and the reserved beef and stir. Simmer for another 8 minutes or more, stirring now and again, until the sauce thickens and takes on flavour. Add the remaining coriander and stir.
5. As directed by the manufacturer, cook the spaghetti.
6. Save 1½ cups of water after straining the pasta. Place the spaghetti and saved pasta water in the pan with the sauce over medium-high heat.
7. Using tongs, toss spaghetti in sauce for three minutes. Add Parmesan cheese to the dish.

Per Serving:

Calories: 413, Fat: 8 g, Carbs: 57 g, Protein: 4 g

36.   Classic Spaghetti Aglio E Olio

Time: 15 minutes | Serves 2

Ingredients:

- 1 lb. spaghetti
- ½ cup extra-virgin olive oil
- 6 cloves garlic, thinly sliced

- ½ teaspoon red pepper flakes (adjust to taste)
- Salt, to taste
- Fresh parsley, chopped (optional)

Method:

1. To start, fill a large pot with water and add a generous amount of salt. Bring the water to a boil. Next, proceed to cook the spaghetti following the guidelines provided on the package until it reaches the desired al dente texture.
2. Before proceeding to drain the spaghetti, it is important to remember to reserve 1/2 cup of the pasta cooking water for later use.
3. While the pasta cooks, heat olive oil in a skillet over medium heat. Sauté the garlic and red pepper flakes in the skillet, stirring regularly, until the garlic turns golden brown and releases a fragrant aroma. This process typically takes about 2-3 minutes.
4. After removing the skillet from the heat, place the cooked pasta into the skillet. Coat the pasta thoroughly in the garlic-infused oil by tossing it.
5. If the pasta appears dry, gradually add small amounts of the reserved pasta cooking water until you achieve the desired consistency.
6. Season the pasta with salt to your liking and toss it once more to ensure proper blending. Serve the spaghetti aglio e olio hot, garnished with fresh parsley if desired.

Per Serving:

Calories: 550 kcal, Fat: 27 g, Carbs: 65 grams, Protein: 11 g

37.   Pasta and Chickpea Soup

Time: 15 minutes | Serves 2

Ingredients:

- 2 tablespoons olive oil
- 1 garlic clove, minced
- 1 cup canned chickpeas, drained and rinsed
- ½ cup small pasta shapes

- 1 small onion, finely chopped
- 1 small carrot, peeled and diced
- 1 small celery stalk, diced
- 2 cups vegetable broth
- 1 cup water
- ½ teaspoon dried thyme
- Salt and black pepper, to taste
- 1 tablespoon chopped fresh parsley
- Grated Parmesan cheese

Method:

1. Heat the olive oil in a large pot over medium heat. Add the onion, garlic, carrot, and celery.
2. Cook, stirring occasionally, until the vegetables are softened, about 5 minutes.
3. Add the drained chickpeas, vegetable broth, water, and thyme. Bring the mixture to a boil.
4. Once boiling, reduce the heat to low and simmer for 10 minutes.
5. Add the pasta to the pot and continue to simmer until the pasta is tender, about 10 more minutes. Season the soup with salt and black pepper to taste.
6. Serve the soup hot, garnished with chopped parsley and grated Parmesan cheese if desired.

Per Serving

Calories: 307; Fat: 8g; Carbs: 43.6g; Protein: 12g

38.   Lemon Garlic Pasta

Time: 15 minutes | Serves 2

Ingredients:

- 12 ounces' spaghetti
- 3 tablespoons olive oil
- 4 cloves garlic, minced
- ¼ teaspoon red pepper flakes

- Salt, to taste
- Juice and zest of 1 large lemon
- ¼ cup chopped fresh parsley
- Grated Parmesan cheese, for serving (optional)

Method:

1. Cook the spaghetti according to the instructions provided on the package until it reaches the desired al dente texture. After cooking, drain the spaghetti and keep it aside for future use.
2. In a large skillet over medium heat, warm the olive oil until it reaches the desired temperature.
3. Next, add the diced onion, carrots, and celery to the skillet. Sauté the vegetables for 5-7 minutes until they begin to soften. Season with salt to taste.
4. Combine the cooked spaghetti with the garlic-infused oil in the skillet and thoroughly toss to ensure that the pasta is evenly coated. Pour the lemon juice over the pasta, then sprinkle the lemon zest on top.
5. Toss the pasta once more to ensure that the flavors are evenly distributed. Continue cooking the mixture for an additional 2-3 minutes, gently stirring it, until the pasta is heated through and reaches the desired temperature.
6. Take the mixture off the heat and incorporate the chopped fresh parsley by stirring it in. Serve the lemon garlic pasta hot, garnished with grated Parmesan cheese if desired.

Per Serving:

Calories: 350 kcal, Fat: 11 g, Carbs: 54 g, Protein: 9 grams

39.   Pesto Pasta

Time: 15 minutes | Serves 2

Ingredients:

- 12 oz. fettuccine or pasta of choice
- 2 cups fresh basil leaves, packed
- ½ cup pine nuts, lightly toasted

- 2 cloves garlic
- ½ cup grated Parmesan cheese
- ½ cup extra-virgin olive oil
- Salt and pepper, to taste
- Fresh basil leaves, chopped (for garnish, optional)

Method:

1. Cook pasta until al dente according to package instructions.
2. Drain cooked pasta and set aside.
3. In a food processor, combine basil leaves, pine nuts, garlic, and Parmesan cheese until finely chopped.
4. Gradually add olive oil while processing until a smooth paste forms. Season with salt and pepper.
5. Heat olive oil in a skillet over medium heat. Add cooked pasta to the skillet and toss to coat with oil.
6. Add desired amount of pesto sauce to the skillet and mix well. Cook for 2-3 minutes until pasta is heated through.
7. Garnish with fresh basil leaves before serving hot.

Per Serving

Calories: 600 kcal, Fat: 47 g, Carbs: 38 g, Protein: 12 g

40.   Vegan Carbonara

Time: 15 minutes | Serves 2

Ingredients:

For the Egg Sauce:

- 1/2 cup raw cashews
- 1/2 cup nutritional yeast
- 1 teaspoon turmeric
- 1 tablespoon Dijon mustard
- ½ teaspoon garlic powder

- ½ teaspoon onion powder
- ½ teaspoon black salt
- 1 cup of soy milk or any non-dairy milk

For the Pasta:

- 8 oz. spaghetti dry
- For the Mushrooms:
- 1 tablespoon vegan butter
- 2 cups mushrooms sliced
- 2 teaspoons crushed garlic
- ½ teaspoon smoked paprika
- ½ teaspoon sea salt
- ½ teaspoon black pepper

For Serving:

- Fresh chopped parsley

Method:

1. Blend ingredients for egg sauce until smooth. Set aside for later use.
2. Cook spaghetti al dente as per package instructions. Drain and set aside.
3. Heat vegan butter in skillet over medium heat. Cook mushrooms for 5-7 minutes until golden-brown.
4. Add garlic, smoked paprika, salt, and pepper. Cook for 2-3 minutes until fragrant.
5. Stir in egg sauce, cook for 2-3 minutes to thicken slightly. Add spaghetti, toss to coat evenly.
6. Cook for another 2-3 minutes until heated through.
7. Off heat, garnish with chopped parsley. Serve hot.

Per Serving

Calories: 400 kcal, Fat: 12 g, Carbs: 60 g, Protein: 15 g

Side & Appetizers

41.   Spicy Wilted Greens with Garlic

Time: 15 minutes | Serves 2

Ingredients:

- 1 tablespoon olive oil
- 2 garlic cloves, minced
- 3 cups sliced greens (kale, spinach, chard, beet greens, dandelion greens, or a combination)
- Pinch salt
- Pinch red pepper flakes (or more to taste)

Method:

1. Heat the olive oil in a sauté pan over medium-high heat.
2. Add garlic and sauté for 30 seconds, or just until it's fragrant.
3. Add the greens, salt, and pepper flakes and stir to combine.
4. Let the greens wilt, but do not overcook.
5. Remove the pan from the heat and serve.

Per Serving:

Calories: 91; fat: 7g; carbs: 7g; Protein: 1g

42.   Roasted Broccolini with Garlic and Romano

Time: 15 minutes | Serves 2

Ingredients:

- 1 bunch broccolini (about 5 ounces)

- 1 tablespoon olive oil
- ½ teaspoon garlic powder
- ¼ teaspoon salt
- 2 tablespoons grated Romano cheese.

Method:

1. Preheat the oven to 400°F and set the oven rack to the middle position. Line a sheet pan with parchment paper or foil.
2. Slice the tough ends off the broccolini and place in a medium bowl. Add the olive oil, garlic powder, and salt and toss to combine. Arrange broccolini on the lined sheet pan.
3. Roast for 7 minutes, flipping pieces over halfway through the roasting time.
4. Remove the pan from the oven and sprinkle the cheese over the broccolini. With a pair of tongs, carefully flip the pieces over to coat all sides.
5. Return to the oven for another 2 to 3 minutes, or until the cheese melts and starts to turn golden.

Per Serving:

Calories: 114; Fat: 9g; Carbs: 5g; Protein: 4g

43.   White Beans with Rosemary, Sage, And Garlic

Time: 10 minutes | Serves 2

Ingredients:

- 1 tablespoon olive oil
- 2 garlic cloves, minced
- 1 (15-ounce) can white cannellini beans, drained and rinsed
- ¼ teaspoon dried sage
- 1 teaspoon minced fresh rosemary (from 1 sprig) plus
- 1 whole fresh rosemary sprig
- ½ cup low-sodium chicken stock Salt

Method:

1. Heat the olive oil in a sauté pan over medium-high heat. Add the garlic and sauté for 30 seconds.
2. Add the beans, sage, minced and whole rosemary, and chicken stock and bring the mixture to a boil.
3. Reduce the heat to medium and simmer the beans for 10 minutes, or until most of the liquid is evaporated. If desired, mash some of the beans with a fork to thicken them.
4. Season with salt. Remove the rosemary sprig before serving

Per Serving:

Calories: 155; Fat: 7g; Carbs: 17g; Protein: 6g

44. Moroccan-Style Couscous

Time: 15 minutes | Serves 2

Ingredients:

- 1 tablespoon olive oil
- ¾ cup couscous

- ¼ teaspoon garlic powder
- ¼ teaspoon salt
- ¼ teaspoon cinnamon
- 1 cup water
- 2 tablespoons raisins
- 2 tablespoons minced dried apricots
- 2 teaspoons minced fresh parsley

Method:

1. Heat the olive oil in a saucepan over medium-high heat. Add the couscous, garlic powder, salt, and cinnamon. Stir for 1 minute to toast the couscous and spices.
2. Add the water, raisins, and apricots and bring the mixture to a boil.

3. Cover the pot and turn off the heat. Let the couscous sit for 4 to 5 minutes and then fluff it with a fork.
4. Add parsley and season with additional salt or spices as needed.

Per Serving:

Calories: 338; Fat: 8g; Carbs: 59g, Protein: 9g

45.　　Grilled Broccoli Rabe

Time: 15 minutes | Serves 2

Ingredients:

- 1 bunch broccoli rabe, trimmed
- 1 tablespoon olive oil
- 1 tablespoon lemon juice
- ¼ teaspoon chili flakes Kosher
- salt, to taste

Method:

1. In a large mixing bowl, combine the broccoli rabe, olive oil, lemon juice, chili flakes, and salt.
2. Heat a large nonstick grill pan over medium heat.
3. Grill the broccoli rabe for 3-5 minutes per side.
4. Serve warm.

Per Serving:

Calories 82, Fat 7g, Carbs 3g, Protein 2g

46.　　Grilled Radicchio with Blue Cheese

Time: 10 minutes | Serves 2

Ingredients:

- 2 tablespoons olive oil
- 2 tablespoons balsamic vinegar
- ½ teaspoon Dijon mustard
- Salt and pepper, to taste
- 1 head radicchio, cut into quarters
- 2 tablespoons pistachio nuts, chopped
- 2 tablespoons crumbled blue cheese

Method:

1. In a large mixing bowl, combine the radicchio, olive oil, balsamic vinegar, Dijon mustard, salt, and pepper.
2. Heat a grill pan or an outdoor grill over medium heat.
3. Grill the radicchio for 3-4 minutes per side.
4. Serve with a sprinkle of chopped pistachios and blue cheese.

Per Serving:

Calories 62, Fat 6g, Carbs 1g, Protein 1g

47.   Roasted Garlicky Kale

Time: 10 minutes | Serves 2

Ingredients:

- 2 large bunches Tuscan kale, chopped with tough ribs removed
- 4-6 garlic cloves, minced
- Salt and pepper, to taste
- Pinch of ground cumin Pinch of cayenne pepper
- ¼ cup olive oil 2 tablespoons balsamic vinegar

Method:

1. Preheat oven to 350°F (177°C).
2. Line a baking sheet with parchment paper.
3. In a large mixing bowl, combine the chopped kale, garlic, salt, pepper, cumin, cayenne pepper, olive oil, and balsamic vinegar.

4. Spread the tossed kale on the prepared baking sheet.
5. Roast for 15 minutes. Serve warm.

Per Serving:

Calories 258, Fat 25g, Carbs 8g, Protein 2g

48.   Ginger and Orange Rice

Time: 15 minutes | Serves 2

Ingredients:

- 2 tablespoons olive oil
- 2 garlic cloves, minced
- Juice of 1 orange
- ½ cup water 2 teaspoons grated ginger
- ½ cup rice
- 2 teaspoons brown sugar
- Salt and pepper, to taste
- 1 tablespoon soy sauce

Method:

1. Heat the olive oil in a large saucepan over medium heat. Add the minced garlic. Cook for 1 minute, stirring frequently.
2. Add the rice, ginger, orange juice, and water.
3. Cover and cook for 10-15 minutes over low heat.
4. Fluff up the cooked rice. Stir in the brown sugar, salt, pepper, and soy sauce.
5. Serve warm.

Per Serving:

Calories 315, Fat 14g, Carbs 42g, Protein 4g

49.   Couscous with Olives and Feta Cheese

Time: 15 minutes | Serves 2

Ingredients:

- 2 tablespoons olive oil
- 1 small onion, diced
- 2 garlic cloves, minced
- ½ cup kalamata olives, pitted and diced
- 1 cup cherry tomatoes, halved
- 1 cup couscous
- 1 cup low-sodium vegetable broth
- 1 tablespoon chopped basil
- 2 ounces' feta cheese, crumbled

Method:

1. Heat the olive oil in a medium saucepan over medium heat.
2. Add the onion and garlic. Cook for 2 minutes, stirring regularly.
3. Add the couscous and vegetable broth, stirring to combine. Cover and cook for 10 minutes over low heat.
4. Fluff up the couscous with a fork. Stir in the cherry tomatoes and kalamata olives. Top with the feta cheese before serving.

Per Serving:

Calories 360, fat 24g, carbs 24g, Protein 9g

50.   Roasted Zucchini

Time: 15 minutes | Serves 2

Ingredients:

- 1 medium zucchini, diced
- Salt and pepper. to taste
- ¼ tsp. cumin

- 1 Tbsp. olive oil, divided
- 1 Tbsp. lemon juice
- 1 garlic clove, minced
- 2 Tbsp. fresh dill, chopped
- 1 Tbsp. fresh basil, chopped
- ½ cup feta cheese, crumbled

Method:

1. Preheat an oven to 425°F. Season zucchini with salt, pepper, cumin, and olive oil.
2. Place zucchini rings in a single layer on a baking sheet. Bake for 10–15 minutes, flipping once.
3. Transfer baked zucchini to a serving plate. Sprinkle with crumbled feta cheese, lemon juice, garlic, and chopped herbs.
4. Serve with roasted pork chops, fried potato, or grilled salmon.

Per Serving:

Calories: 150, Carbs: 9.1 g, Fat: 9 g, Protein: 5 g

51. Italian Fried Calamari

Time: 5 minutes | Serves 2

Ingredients:

- 1 lb. squid rings (cut the squid into circles)
- A neutral-flavored oil with a high smoke point for frying (such as peanut oil or refined coconut oil)
- 4 medium eggs
- 2/3 cup unbleached flour for all purposes
- 4 tablespoons semolina
- 1 lemon (cut into pieces)
- Salt

Method:

1. Rinse squid pieces in running water and dry thoroughly with paper towels.
2. Heat a few inches of the oil in a large, high-walled pan with a thick bottom over medium heat or 350°F.
3. Place the flour in a shallow bowl. Beat the eggs in a large bowl. Place the semolina in a small bowl.
4. Dip the squid rings in the flour and shake them to remove the excess. Dip in the egg and then in the semolina before frying them in the hot oil.
5. Fry calamari in different batches to avoid overcrowding until you get a crisp, light brown texture, about one to two minutes.
6. Transfer the fried squid to a dish with absorbent paper to drain. Season with salt and serve with lemon slices.

Per Serving:

Calories: 333; Fat: 11g; Carbs: 29g; Protein: 29g

52.   Roasted Chickpeas

Time: 15 minutes | Serves 2

Ingredients:

- 1/3 teaspoon salt

- ¼ teaspoon dried oregano
- ¼ teaspoon garlic powder
- ¼ teaspoon ground black pepper
- 1 tablespoon olive oil
- 1 teaspoon red wine vinegar
- 1 teaspoon lemon juice

Method:

1. Switch on the oven, set it to 218 degrees C or 425 degrees F, and let it preheat.
2. Take a baking tray, line it with parchment paper, arrange the chickpeas on it in a single layer.

3. Place the baking sheet in the oven. Roast the chickpeas for 10 minutes until tender-crisp and golden brown, tossing halfway through.
4. Take a large bowl, place salt, black pepper, oregano, garlic powder, black pepper, oil, red wine vinegar, and lemon juice. Stir until combined.
5. Add the roasted chickpeas, toss until well mixed, and then layer the chickpeas mixture on the baking tray.
6. Return it into the oven and then continue roasting for 5 minutes or brown. When done, spoon the mixture into the serving bowl, and serve.

Per Serving

Calories: 238; Fat: 7.8g; Carbs: 32g; Protein: 10.6g

53.   Baked Beet Chips

Time: 15 minutes | Serves 2

Ingredients:

- 2 large beets, trimmed, scrubbed, sliced
- ½ tablespoon dried chives
- ½ tablespoon salt
- 1 tablespoon olive oil

Method:

1. Switch on the oven, set it to 204 degrees C or 400 degrees F, and let it preheat.
2. Meanwhile, take a baking tray, drizzle oil, spread it all around to grease the tray, and then set it aside until required.
3. Place the beets on the prepared baking tray in a single layer and then bake for 10 minutes, until crispy.
4. Take a small bowl, place salt and chives, and stir until mixed.
5. When the beet chips have baked, sprinkle the prepared salt mixture on top, and let the beets cool at room temperature. Toss the beet chips and then serve.

Per Serving

Calories: 110.4; Fat: 2.4g; Carbs: 14g; Protein: 2.6g

54.   **Roasted Pumpkin Seeds**

Time: 15 minutes | Serves 2

Ingredients:

- 1 cup pumpkin seeds, rinsed, dried
- ¼ teaspoon salt
- ¼ teaspoon ground black pepper
- 1 teaspoon olive oil

Method:

1. Switch on the oven, set it to 204 degrees C or 400 degrees F, and let it preheat.
2. Meanwhile, take a large bowl, place pumpkin seeds in it, drizzle with oil, toss until well coated, then stir in salt and black pepper until well mixed.
3. Take a baking sheet, line it with a sheet of parchment, sprinkle the pumpkin seeds on top in a single layer, and then bake for 12-15 minutes until crispy.
4. When done, let the pumpkin seeds rest for 5 minutes and then serve.

Per Serving

Calories: 169; Fat: 14g; Carbs: 4.3g; Protein: 8.8g

55.   **Beet Hummus**

Time: 5 minutes | Serves 2

Ingredients:

- 1 small beet, cooked, peeled, and chopped
- ¼ teaspoon minced garlic
- ½ cup chickpeas, canned, drained, and rinsed
- ¼ teaspoon salt

- ¼ teaspoon ground black pepper
- 2 tablespoons olive oil
- 1 teaspoon tahini
- 2 teaspoons lemon juice

Method:

1. In a food processor, place chickpeas and add oil, beet, lemon juice, tahini and garlic.
2. Pulse for 1 minute or more until well combined, add salt and black pepper and pulse until well-mixed and smooth.
3. When done, spoon the prepared hummus into the serving bowl, and serve with favorite crackers and vegetable slices.

Per Serving

Calories: 112; Fat: 7g; Carbs: 10g; Protein: 2.1g

56. Tuna Salad Sandwiches

Time: 15 minutes | Serves 2

Ingredients:

- 6 oz. white tuna, drained
- 1 roasted red pepper, diced
- Juice of 1 lemon
- ½ small red onion, diced
- 10 olives, pitted and finely chopped
- ¼ cup plain Greek yogurt
- 1 tbsp parsley, chopped
- Salt and freshly ground pepper, to taste
- 1 tbsp olive oil
- 4 pieces whole-grain bread

Method:

1. Combine all ingredients, except the bread and olive oil, in a medium bowl, then stir to mix well.
2. Heat the olive oil in a non-stick skillet over medium-high heat.
3. Toast the bread in the skillet for 2 to 4 minutes or until golden brown. Flip the bread halfway through the cooking time.
4. Lastly, assemble the bread with the mixture to make the sandwich and serve warm.

Per Serving

Calories: 270; Fat: 15g; Carbs: 26g; Protein: 17g

57.   Peach Caprese Skewers

Time: 5 minutes | Serves 2

Ingredients:

- 2 medium peaches slices
- 1 cup cherry tomatoes
- ½ cup baby mozzarella balls
- 6 fresh basil leaves

Method:

1. Thread peach slices, tomatoes, mozzarella balls, and basil alternately onto skewers.

Per Serving

Calories: 143; Fat: 5,6g; Carbs: 17.3g; Protein: 7,2g

58.   Hummus

Time: 5 minutes | Serves 2

Ingredients:

- 1 cup cooked chickpeas
- ½ teaspoon minced garlic
- ½ teaspoon salt
- ½ teaspoon lemon pepper seasoning
- 2 teaspoons olive oil
- 2 tablespoons tahini paste
- 2 teaspoons lemon juice
- 2 cubes of ice

Method:

2. Place in a food processor, add the chickpeas and garlic and pulse for 30 seconds or more until smooth and powder-like in consistency.
3. Then add tahini, salt, ice cube, and lemon juice, and pulse until the mixture is well combined and smooth.
4. When done, spoon the hummus into a bowl, drizzle oil on it, sprinkle with the lemon pepper seasoning and serve with favorite crackers and vegetable slices.

Per Serving

Calories: 176; Fat: 8.7g; Carbs: 19.4 g; Protein: 7.2g

59. Eggplant Dip

Time: 10 minutes | Serves 2

Ingredients:

- 1 small eggplant
- 1 small tomato, diced

- 4 tablespoons diced cucumber
- ½ cup parsley leaves
- ½ teaspoon chopped garlic
- ¼ teaspoon salt, divided
- ¼ teaspoon ground black pepper, divided

- ½ teaspoon lemon pepper seasoning

- ¼ teaspoon Aleppo pepper
- 1 tablespoon tahini paste
- 1 tablespoon olive oil
- ¾ tablespoon yogurt, low-fat, unsweetened
- ½ tablespoon lemon juice, divided

Method:

1. Turn the stove on medium heat, place the eggplant on the burner, and then cook for 8 to 10 minutes until charred, rotate occasionally.
2. When done, transfer the eggplant to a plate, let it cool, and then peel it.
3. Place the peeled eggplant on a drainer, let it rest for 3 minutes to drain any liquid, and then place in a food processor.
4. Add garlic, tahini, yogurt, lemon juice, salt, black pepper, lemon pepper seasoning, and Aleppo pepper, and then pulse for 1 minute until smooth.
5. Spoon the prepared dip into a serving bowl, cover the bowl with its lid, place in a refrigerator and let it rest for 30 minutes.
6. Meanwhile, take a medium bowl, add tomato, cucumber, parsley, salt, and black pepper, drizzle with oil and lemon juice, and stir until well mixed.
7. After 30 minutes, let the eggplant dip rest at room temperature for 10 minutes, top with the prepared tomato mixture, and then serve with crackers.

Per Serving

Calories: 138; Fat: 9.4g; Carbs: 13.8g; Protein: 2.4g

60.　　Artichoke Crab

Time: 10 minutes | Serves 2

Ingredients:

- 7 ounces' baguette, cut into slices
- ½ cup Greek yogurt
- 2 tablespoons flat-leaf parsley, chopped
- 1 teaspoon lemon zest
- 1 tablespoon lemon juice

- ¼ teaspoon garlic powder
- Salt and pepper, to taste
- ¼ teaspoon cayenne pepper
- 2 ounces Gruyere cheese, shredded
- 1 ounces grated parmesan cheese
- 7 ounces can artichoke hearts, rinsed, drained, and roughly diced
- 4 ounces can lump crab meat, drained and crumbled

Method:

1. Slice the baguette into 1-inch slices. Toast the slices in a large skillet over medium heat, about 4-5 minutes per side (add 1-2 tablespoons of olive oil if you like a crispier texture).
2. Remove from heat and keep the bread in the hot skillet to keep warm.
3. In a large mixing bowl, combine the Greek yogurt, parsley, lemon zest, lemon juice, garlic powder, salt, pepper, cayenne pepper, shredded cheese, parmesan, diced artichoke hearts, and crumbled crab meat.
4. Finally, top the crab and artichoke mixture over each crostini. Transfer to a serving plate and serve.

Per Serving

Calories 456, fat 7 g, carbs 65 g, Protein 30 g

Soup & Salad

61.   Creamy Tomato Hummus Soup

Time: 10 minutes | Serves 2

Ingredients:

- 1 (14.5-ounce) can crushed tomatoes with basil
- 1 cup roasted red pepper hummus
- 2 cups low-sodium chicken stock Salt
- ¼ cup fresh basil leaves, thinly sliced (optional, for garnish)
- Garlic croutons (optional, for garnish)

Method:

1. Combine the canned tomatoes, hummus, and chicken stock in a blender and blend until smooth.
2. Pour the mixture into a saucepan and bring it to a boil.
3. Season with salt and fresh basil if desired.
4. Serve with garlic croutons as a garnish, if desired.

Per Serving:

Calories: 148; fat: 6g; carbs: 19g; Protein: 5g

62.   Mediterranean Tomato Hummus Soup

Time: 10 minutes | Serves 2

Ingredients:

- 1 (14.5-ounce) can crushed tomatoes with basil
- 2 cups low-sodium chicken stock
- 1 cup roasted red pepper hummus
- Salt, to taste
- ¼ cup thinly sliced fresh basil leaves, for garnish (optional)

Method:

1. Combine the canned tomatoes, hummus, and chicken stock in a blender and blend until smooth.
2. Pour the mixture into a saucepan and bring it to a boil.
3. Season with salt to taste.
4. Serve garnished with the fresh basil, if desired.

Per Serving

Calories: 147, Fat: 6.2g, Carbs: 20.1g, Protein: 5.2g

63.   Chickpea Soup with Pasta

Time: 15 minutes | Serves 2

Ingredients:

- 15 ounces' cherry tomatoes, canned, drained
- ½ teaspoon crushed dried rosemary
- 1 teaspoon chopped garlic
- 12 ounces cooked chickpeas, divided
- 3 ounces' whole-wheat pasta
- ¼ teaspoon ground black pepper
- 1 teaspoon olive oil
- 3 tablespoons grated parmesan cheese, low-fat
- 15 ounces' beef broth, sodium-reduced
- 1 cup water

Method:

1. Take a medium pot, place it over low heat, add oil and when hot, add garlic and cook for a minute until fragrant and golden.
2. Then add tomatoes, and rosemary, simmer for 3 minutes and then take a potato masher to crush the tomatoes.
3. Pour in the beef broth and water, turn on medium-high heat and bring the soup to a boil.

4. Take a medium bowl, place half of the chickpeas, and with a potato masher, crush the chickpeas.
5. Add the crushed chickpeas into the soup along with the pasta and black pepper and stir until combined.
6. Let the soup simmer for 7 minutes or until the pasta has cooked, then add the remaining chickpeas into the soup, and stir until well mixed. When done, spoon the prepared soup into a serving bowl, and serve.

Per Serving

Calories: 307; Fat: 4.8g; Carbs: 53.6g; Protein: 13.6g

64.   Nettle Soup

Time: 15 minutes | Serves 2

Ingredients:

- 1.2 lb. young top shoots of nettles, well washed
- 3 tbsp sunflower oil
- 2 potatoes, diced small
- 1 bunch of green onions, coarsely chopped
- 2 cups hot water
- 1 tsp salt

Method:

1. Clean the young nettles, wash and cook them in slightly salted water.
2. Drain, rinse, drain again and then chop or pass through a sieve.
3. Sauté the chopped green onions and potatoes in the oil until the potatoes start to color a little.
4. Turn off the heat, add the nettles, then gradually stir in the water. Stir well, then simmer until the potatoes are cooked through.

Per Serving:

Calories 441, Fat 19.7g, Carbs 7.8g, Fiber 3.1g, Protein 15g

65.   Spanish Cold Soup (Ajo Blanco)

Time: 15 minutes | Serves 2

Ingredients:

- 1 cup almonds, blanched
- 2 cloves garlic
- 2 slices of bread, crust removed
- 3 tablespoons olive oil
- 2 tablespoons sherry vinegar
- 3 cups cold water
- Salt to taste

Method:

1. Soak bread in water for a few minutes, then squeeze in excess water.
2. Combine almonds, soaked bread, garlic, and salt in a blender.
3. Blend until smooth, gradually adding olive oil and sherry vinegar.
4. Add cold water to achieve the desired consistency.
5. Chill in the refrigerator. Serve the soup cold, garnished with a drizzle of olive oil.

Per Serving

Calories: 300, Fat: 22g, Carbs: 18g, Protein: 10g

66.   Miso Soup

Time: 15 minutes | Serves 2

Ingredients:

- 4 cups water

- 2 tsp. of dashi granules
- 3 tbsp. of miso paste

- 1 (8-oz.) package of silken tofu, diced
- 2 green onions, sliced diagonally into 1/2-inch pieces

Method:

1. Bring the mixture of water and dashi granules to a boil in a medium saucepan over medium-high heat.
2. Melt miso paste over medium heat while whisking. Add the tofu after stirring.
3. Green onions should be cut into layers and then added to the soup.
4. Before serving, gently simmer for 2 to 3 minutes.

Per Serving

Calories: 196; Fat: 6g; Carbs: 13g; Protein: 16g

67.   Fig and Arugula Salad

Time: 15 minutes | Serves 2

Ingredients:

- 3 cups arugula

- 4 fresh, ripe figs (or 4 to 6 dried figs), stemmed and sliced
- 2 tablespoons olive oil
- 3 very thin slices prosciutto, trimmed and sliced lengthwise into 1-inch strips
- ¼ cup pecan halves, lightly toasted
- 2 tablespoons crumbled blue cheese
- 1 to 2 tablespoons balsamic glaze (see Strawberry Caprese Skewers)

Method:

1. In a large bowl, toss the arugula and figs with the olive oil.
2. Place the prosciutto on a microwave-safe plate and heat it on high in the microwave for 60 seconds, or until it just starts to crisp.
3. Add the crisped prosciutto, pecans, and blue cheese to the bowl. Toss the salad lightly.
4. Drizzle with the balsamic glaze.

Calories: 519; Fat: 38g; Carbs: 30g; Protein: 20g

68.   Watermelon Feta Salad

Time: 10 minutes | Serves 2

Ingredients:

- 3 cups packed arugula
- 2½ cups watermelon, cut into bite-size cubes
- 2 ounces' feta cheese, crumbled
- 2 tablespoons balsamic glaze

Method:

1. Divide the arugula between two plates.
2. Divide the watermelon cubes between the beds of arugula. 3.Sprinkle 1 ounce of the feta over each salad.
3. Drizzle about 1 tablespoon of the glaze (or more if desired) over each salad.
4. I don't think this salad needs any salt because the feta is salty enough, but feel free to add a pinch if you like.

Per Serving:

Calories: 159; Fat: 7g; Carbs: 21g; Protein: 6g

69.   Citrus Fennel Salad

Time: 15 minutes | Serves 2

Ingredients:

For the dressing

- 2 tablespoons fresh orange juice

- 3 tablespoons olive oil

- 1 tablespoon blood orange vinegar, other orange vinegar, or cider vinegar
- 1 tablespoon honey Salt Freshly ground black pepper

For the salad

- 2 cups packed baby kale
- 1 medium navel or blood orange, segmented
- ½ small fennel bulb, stems and leaves removed, sliced into matchsticks
- 3 tablespoons toasted pecans, chopped
- 2 ounces goat cheese, crumbled

Method:

Combine the orange juice, olive oil, vinegar, and honey in a small bowl and whisk to combine. Season with salt and pepper. Set the dressing aside.

Divide the baby kale, orange segments, fennel, pecans, and goat cheese evenly between two plates.

Drizzle half of the dressing over each salad.

Per Serving:

Calories: 502; Fat: 39g; Carbs: 31g; Protein: 13g

70.   Mixed Salad with Balsamic Honey Dressing

Time: 15 minutes | Serves 2

Ingredients:

Dressing:

- ¼ cup balsamic vinegar
- ¼ cup olive oil
- 1 tablespoon honey
- 1 teaspoon Dijon mustard
- ¼ teaspoon garlic powder

- ¼ teaspoon salt, or more to taste

- Pinch freshly ground black pepper

Salad:

- 4 cups chopped red leaf lettuce
- ½ cup cherry or grape tomatoes, halved
- ½ English cucumber, sliced in quarters lengthwise and then cut into bite-size pieces
- Any combination fresh, torn herbs (parsley, oregano, basil, or chives)
- 1 tablespoon roasted sunflower seeds

Method:

1. Combine the vinegar, olive oil, honey, mustard, garlic powder, salt, and pepper in a jar with a lid. Shake well.
2. In a large bowl, combine the lettuce, tomatoes, cucumber, and herbs. Toss well.
3. Pour all or as much dressing as desired over the tossed salad and toss again to coat the salad with dressing.
4. Top with the sunflower seeds before serving.

Per Serving

Calories: 337, Fat: 26.1g, Carbs: 22.2g, Protein: 4.2g

71.   Citrus Salad with Kale and Fennel

Time: 10 minutes | Serves 2

Ingredients:

Dressing:

- 3 tablespoons olive oil
- 2 tablespoons fresh orange juice
- 1 tablespoon blood orange vinegar, other orange vinegar, or cider vinegar
- 1 tablespoon honey
- Salt and freshly ground black pepper, to taste

Salad:

- 2 cups packed baby kale
- 1 medium navel or blood orange, segmented
- ½ small fennel bulb, stems and leaves removed, sliced into matchsticks
- 3 tablespoons toasted pecans, chopped
- 2 ounces' goat cheese, crumbled

Method:

1. Mix the olive oil, orange juice, vinegar, and honey in a small bowl and whisk to combine.
2. Season with salt and pepper to taste. Set aside.
3. Divide the baby kale, orange segments, fennel, pecans, and goat cheese evenly between two plates.
4. Drizzle half of the dressing over each salad, and serve.

Per Serving

Calories: 503, Fat: 39.1g, Carbs: 31.2g, Protein: 13.2g

72.   Cucumber and Tomato Salad

Time: 10 minutes | Serves 2

Ingredients:

- Salt and black pepper, to taste
- 1 tablespoon fresh lemon juice
- ½ onion, chopped
- ½ cucumber, peeled and diced
- 1 tomato, chopped
- 2 cups spinach

Method:

1. In a salad bowl, mix the onion, cucumbers, and tomatoes.
2. Season with pepper and salt to taste.

3. Add the lemon juice and mix well.
4. Add the spinach, toss to coat, serve and enjoy.
5. Top with feta cheese and chickpeas.

Per Serving:

Calories 70.3; Fat 0.3g; Carbs 8.9g; Protein 2.2g

73. Pear Salad with Roquefort Cheese

Time: 10 minutes | Serves 2

Ingredients:

- 1 leaf lettuce, torn into bite-sized pieces
- 3 pears - peeled, cored and diced
- 5 ounces Roquefort, crumbled
- 1 avocado - peeled, seeded and diced
- ½ cup chopped green onions
- ¼ cup white sugar
- ½ cup pecan nuts
- 1/3 cup olive oil
- 3 tablespoons red wine vinegar
- 1 ½ teaspoon of white sugar
- 1 ½ teaspoon of prepared mustard
- ½ teaspoon of salted black pepper
- 1 clove of garlic

Method:

1. Mix ¼ cup of sugar with the pecans in a large skillet over medium-low heat.
2. Continue to stir gently until the sugar has melted and is caramelized with pecans.
3. Carefully transfer the nuts to wax paper. Allow to cool and break into pieces.
4. Mix vinaigrette oil, vinegar, 1 1/2 teaspoon of sugar, mustard, chopped garlic, salt, and pepper.
5. Add lettuce, pears, blue cheese, avocado, and green onions in a large bowl.

6. Pour vinaigrette over salad, sprinkle with pecans and serve.

Per Serving:

Calories: 426; Fat: 31.6 g; Carbs: 33.1 g; Protein: 8 g

74.   Grilled Eggplant Salad

Time: 15 minutes | Serves 2

Ingredients:

- 1 large eggplant
- 1 diced plum tomato
- 1 ½ tsp red wine vinegar
- ½ tsp kosher salt to taste
- ½ tsp chopped fresh oregano
- 1 finely chopped garlic cloves
- 3 tbsp. extra virgin olive oil
- 3 tbsp. chopped parsley
- Black pepper to taste
- Capers

Method:

1. Heat the grill medium-high.

2. Prick eggplant with a fork all over, place on the grill and close the lid; cook for 15 minutes, occasionally turning, until eggplant is very soft and the skin is blistered.
3. Pull out the insides of the eggplants when they are fairly fresh and coarsely chop them.
4. Transfer the tomatoes, vinegar, salt, oregano and garlic to a bowl and toss.
5. Stir in the parsley and oil; season with more salt and pepper if necessary. If you like them, garnish them with capers. Use warm pita bread to serve.

Per Serving:

Calories: 252; Fat: 16.4g; Carbs: 18.8g; Protein: 6.3g

75. Mushroom Salad with Blue Cheese and Arugula

Time: 10 minutes | Serves 2

Ingredients:

- 1-pound portobello sliced mushrooms
- ¼ cup of extra virgin olive oil
- ¼ cup of red wine
- ¼ tsp salt
- ¼ tsp pepper
- 1 tsp thyme
- 2 cups of arugula
- 2 medium tomatoes cut into wedges
- 1/4 of a sliced thinly red onion
- ¼ cup of blue cheese
- ½ cup of croutons
- ⅓ cup of balsamic vinegar

Method:

1. Heat olive oil in a medium-hot skillet. Stir in the mushrooms and sauté for about 1 minute.
2. Add the red wine, salt, thyme, and pepper. Sauté, frequently stirring, until mushrooms have absorbed liquid (about 10 minutes).
3. Remove it from the heat. Add the arugula and the tomatoes to a large salad bowl. Arugula is covered with warm mushrooms.
4. Combine the red onion salad, blue cheese, croutons, and balsamic vinegar. Instantly serve.

Per Serving:

Calories 222; Fat 0.6 g; Carbs 58.2 g; Protein 1.3 g

76.   Artichoke Salad

Time: 10 minutes | Serves 2

Ingredients:

- ¼ tsp. crushed red pepper
- ½ tsp. dried oregano
- ½ tsp. dried basil
- 2 Tbsp. olive oil
- ¼ tsp. garlic powder
- 1 cup sun-dried tomatoes, chopped
- 1½ cups marinated artichoke hearts, cut into bite-size pieces
- 1 cup fresh arugula
- ½ cup olives
- salt and pepper, to taste
- ½ Tbsp. white wine vinegar

Method:

1. Combine all the vegetables in a large bowl.
2. Mix the garlic powder, olive oil, rosemary, thyme, pepper, salt, and vinegar in a small bowl.
3. Drizzle dressing over the vegetables and serve.

Per Serving:

Calories: 356, Fat: 32.1 g, Carbs: 10.9 g, Protein: 1 g

77.   Avocado and Cucumber Salad

Time: 10 minutes | Serves 2

Ingredients:

- 1 avocado, peeled, halved and sliced
- ½ red onion, thinly sliced
- 1 large cucumber, halved, sliced

- 3 tbsp. basil pesto
- 2 tbsp. lemon juice

Method:

1. Combine the avocados, onion and cucumber in a bowl.
2. Stir in the basil pesto and serve.

Per Serving:

Calories 169, Fat 144 g, Carbs 11 g, Protein 2 g

78.   Chicken and Broccoli Salad

Time: 10 minutes | Serves 2

Ingredients:

- 2 cooked chicken breasts, diced
- 1 small head broccoli, cut into florets
- 1 cup cherry tomatoes, halved
- 2 tbsp. olive oil
- 2 tbsp. basil pesto

Method:

1. Heat two tablespoons of olive oil in a non-stick frying pan and gently sauté broccoli for 5-6 minutes until tender.
2. broccoli in a large salad bowl. Stir in the chicken and tomatoes.
3. Add the basil pesto, toss to combine and serve.

Per Serving:

Calories 341, Fat 28.7 g, Carbs 12.8g, Protein 11 g

79.   Caprese Salad

Time: 4 minutes | Serves 2

Ingredients:

- 2 tomatoes, sliced
- 2 oz. mozzarella cheese, sliced
- 6-7 fresh basil leaves
- 2 tbsp. extra virgin olive oil
- 1 tbsp. red wine vinegar

Method:

1. In a plate, layer the basil leaves, sliced tomatoes and mozzarella
2. Sprinkle with vinegar and olive oil and serve.

Per Serving:

Calories 127, Fat 3.9 g, Carbs 23.9 g, Protein 14.5 g

80.   Greek Salad with Grilled Chicken

Time: 4 minutes | Serves 2

Ingredients:

- 2 boneless, skinless chicken breasts
- 1 large cucumber, diced
- 2 tomatoes, diced
- ½ red onion, thinly sliced
- 1/4 cup Kalamata olives
- 1/4 cup feta cheese, crumbled
- 2 tablespoons olive oil
- 1 tablespoon red wine vinegar
- 1 teaspoon dried oregano
- Salt and pepper to taste

Method:

1. Preheat the grill to medium-high heat. Season chicken breasts with salt, pepper, and 1 teaspoon dried oregano.

2. Grill chicken for 5 minutes on each side or until fully cooked. Let it rest for 5 minutes, then slice thinly.
3. Combine cucumber, tomatoes, red onion, Kalamata olives, and feta cheese in a large bowl.
4. Whisk together olive oil, red wine vinegar, salt, and pepper in a small bowl. Pour over the salad and toss to combine.
5. Top the salad with sliced grilled chicken. Serve immediately or chill before serving.

Per Serving:

Calories: 350, Fat: 20g, Carbs: 18g Protein: 26g

Vegetable Main

81.   Beet and Carrot Fritters with Yogurt Sauce

Time: 15 minutes | Serves 2

Ingredients:

For the yogurt sauce

- ⅓ cup plain Greek yogurt
- 1 tablespoon freshly squeezed lemon juice
- Zest of ½ lemon
- ¼ teaspoon garlic powder
- ¼ teaspoon salt

For the fritters

- 1 large carrot, peeled
- 1 small potato, peeled
- 1 medium golden or red beet, peeled
- 1 scallion, minced
- 2 tablespoons fresh minced parsley
- ¼ cup brown rice flour or unseasoned bread crumbs
- ¼ teaspoon garlic powder
- ¼ teaspoon salt
- 1 large egg, beaten
- ¼ cup feta cheese, crumbled
- 2 tablespoons olive oil (more if needed)

Method:

1. In a small bowl, mix together the yogurt, lemon juice and zest, garlic powder, and salt. Set aside.
2. Shred the carrot, potato, and beet in a food processor with the shredding blade. You can also use a mandoline with a julienne shredding blade or a vegetable

peeler. Squeeze out any moisture from the vegetables and place them in a large bowl.

3. Add the scallion, parsley, rice flour, garlic powder, salt, and egg. Stir the mixture well to combine. Add the feta cheese and stir briefly, leaving chunks of feta cheese throughout.

4. Heat a large nonstick sauté pan over medium-high heat and add 1 tablespoon of the olive oil.

5. Make the fritters by scooping about 3 tablespoons of the vegetable mixture into your hands and flattening it into a firm disc about 3 inches in diameter.

6. Place 2 fritters at a time in the pan and let them cook for about two minutes. Check to see if the underside is golden, and then flip and repeat on the other side. Remove from the heat, add the rest of the olive oil to the pan, and repeat with the remaining vegetable mixture.

7. To serve, spoon about 1 tablespoon of the yogurt sauce on top of each fritter.

Per Serving:

Calories: 295; Fat: 14g; Carbs: 44g; Protein: 6g

82.   Socca Pan Pizza with Herbed Ricotta, Fresh Tomato, And Balsamic Glaze

Time: 15 minutes | Serves 2

Ingredients:

- 1 cup chickpea flour
- 1 teaspoon baking powder
- ½ teaspoon salt
- ½ teaspoon garlic powder
- ½ teaspoon onion powder
- 1½ teaspoons Italian seasoning herb mix, divided
- 2 tablespoons grated Parmesan Cheese Up to
- 1 cup warm water
- Olive oil, enough to coat the bottom of a skillet
- ½ cup ricotta cheese

- 1 ripe tomato, thinly sliced
- Balsamic glaze

Method:

1. Preheat the oven to 425°F and set the rack to the middle position.
2. While the oven is heating, combine the chickpea flour, baking powder, salt, garlic powder, onion powder, 1 teaspoon of the Italian seasoning herb mix, and the Parmesan cheese in a medium bowl.
3. Add most of the water and whisk to combine. The batter should be a pourable consistency like pancake batter, but not as thin as a crepe batter. You may not need all of the water.
4. Heat a large (10- to 12-inch) nonstick or cast iron skillet on the stovetop over medium-high heat and add the oil.
5. When the pan is hot, pour the batter into the pan and let it cook for a minute, until bubbles start to form. Transfer the pan to the oven and let it cook for 10 minutes, or until the batter starts to turn golden around the edges and looks set.
6. In a small bowl, combine the ricotta cheese and the remaining ½ teaspoon of Italian seasoning herb mix.
7. Remove the pan from the oven and gently spread the ricotta over the crust. Top with the sliced tomatoes and return to the oven for another 2 minutes to let the cheese melt.
8. Use a spatula to remove the dough from the pan. Drizzle it with balsamic glaze, slice, and serve.

Per Serving:

Calories: 318; Fat: 10g; Carbs: 37g; Protein: 20g

83.   Grilled Eggplant Stacks

Time: 10 minutes | Serves 2

Ingredients:

- 1 medium eggplant, cut crosswise into 8 slices

- ¼ teaspoon salt
- 1 teaspoon Italian herb seasoning mix
- 2 tablespoons olive oil
- 1 large tomato, cut into 4 slices
- 4 (1-ounce) slices of buffalo mozzarella
- Fresh Basil, For Garnish

Method:

1. Place the eggplant slices in a colander set in the sink or over a bowl. Sprinkle both sides with the salt. Let the eggplant sit for 15 minutes.
2. While the eggplant is resting, heat the grill to medium-high heat (about 350°F).
3. Pat the eggplant dry with paper towels and place it in a mixing bowl. Sprinkle it with the Italian herb seasoning mix and olive oil. Toss well to coat.
4. Grill the eggplant for 5 minutes, or until it has grill marks and is lightly charred. Flip each eggplant slice over, and grill on the second side for another 5 minutes.
5. Flip the eggplant slices back over and top four of the slices with a slice of tomato and a slice of mozzarella. Top each stack with one of the remaining four slices of eggplant.
6. Turn the grill down to low and cover it to let the cheese melt. Check after 30 seconds and remove when the cheese is soft and mostly melted.
7. Sprinkle with fresh basil slices.

Per Serving:

Calories: 354; Fat: 29g; Carbs: 19g; Protein: 13g

84.   Quick Hummus Bowls

Time: 10 minutes | Serves 2

Ingredients:

- ½ cup hummus
- 16 English cucumber slices
- 1 small red onion, sliced

- 1 cup cherry tomatoes, halved
- ⅔ cup diced and pitted Kalamata olives
- 2 tablespoons crumbled feta cheese
- A handful of baby greens
- ½ cup cooked brown rice
- 1 pita bread, chopped

Method:

1. In a large mixing bowl, combine the rice and greens.
2. Add the hummus, cucumber, red onion, kalamata olives, cherry tomatoes, and feta cheese.
3. Combine well. Serve the dip with the pita bread.

Per Serving:

Calories 477, Fat 13 G, Carbs 76 G, Protein 14 G

85. Easy Veggie Wrap

Time: 15 minutes | Serves 2

Ingredients:

- 7 ounces' chickpeas, drained and rinsed
- 1 celery stalk, diced
- 2 green onions, diced
- 3 tablespoons mayonnaise
- ½ tablespoon Dijon mustard
- ½ tablespoon apple cider vinegar
- ½ teaspoon celery seeds
- Salt and pepper, to taste
- ½ cup hummus
- ¼ red cabbage, thinly sliced
- ½ red bell pepper, cored, seeded, and sliced
- 1 cup chopped lettuce
- 2 large tortillas Directions

1. In a large mixing bowl, use a fork to smash the chickpeas.
2. Add the celery, green onions, mayonnaise, mustard, vinegar, celery seeds, and hummus.
3. Season with salt and pepper. Toss well to combine.
4. Spread the hummus mixture on each tortilla, then arrange the cabbage, pepper, and lettuce on the tortilla.
5. Roll each tortilla into a wrap. Serve fresh.

Per Serving:

Calories 387, Fat 15 G, Carbs 52 G, Protein 12 G

86.   Italian Eggplant Sandwich

Time: 10 minutes | Serves 2

Ingredients:

- 1 medium eggplant, sliced into circles
- Salt and pepper, to taste
- 1 tomato, sliced
- ¼ pound mozzarella cheese, sliced
- ¼ cup pesto
- 3-4 tablespoons olive oil
- 2 pieces' focaccia

Method:

1. Heat the olive oil on a grill pan over medium heat.
2. Add the eggplant slices and cook on each side for 3-4 minutes. Season with salt and pepper.
3. Transfer the grilled eggplant slices to a plate lined with paper towel. Toast the bread in the grill pan on each side for 1-2 minutes.

4. Divide the pesto between each slice of bread. Top with the eggplant and tomato slices. Arrange the mozzarella cheese slices over the eggplant and tomato slices.
5. Top with the other piece of bread spread with the pesto. Serve fresh.

Per Serving:

Calories 698, fat 38g, carbs 74g, Protein 16g

87. Tomato Stuffed with Cheese & Peppers

Time: 15 minutes | Serves 2

Ingredients:

- 2 large tomatoes
- ½ cup mixed bell peppers, finely chopped
- 1 tablespoon olive oil
- 1 garlic cloves, minced
- ½ cup crumbled feta cheese
- 1 tablespoon chopped fresh basil
- Salt and black pepper to taste

Method:

1. Preheat your oven to 375°F (190°C).
2. Slice the tops off the tomatoes and carefully scoop out the seeds and core to create a hollow, leaving the outer walls intact.
3. In a mixing bowl, combine the chopped bell peppers, crumbled feta cheese, chopped basil, and minced garlic. Season with salt and black pepper.
4. Stuff the hollowed-out tomatoes with the cheese and pepper mixture, packing it lightly.
5. Place the stuffed tomatoes in a baking dish and drizzle with olive oil.
6. Bake in the preheated oven for about 15 minutes, or until the tomatoes are tender but still hold their shape.

Per Serving:

Calories: 185, Fat: 10g, Carbs: 8g, Protein: 9g

88.   Spiralized Carrot with Peas

Time: 15 minutes | Serves 2

Ingredients:

- 2 large carrots, spiralized or grated
- ½ cup green peas, fresh or frozen
- 1 garlic clove, minced
- 1 tbsp. olive oil
- Salt and black pepper to taste

Method:

1. Heat the olive oil in a large skillet over medium heat.
2. Add the minced garlic and sauté for about 1 minute until fragrant.
3. Add the spiralized carrots to the skillet and stir to coat with the olive oil and garlic. 4   Cook for about 2 minutes, then add the peas.
4. Continue cooking for another 2-3 minutes, or until the carrots are tender and the peas are heated through.
5. Season with salt and freshly ground black pepper to taste. Serve immediately

Per Serving:

Calories: 117, Fat: 7.3g, Carbs: 12.6g, Protein: 4g

89.   Catalan-Style Spinach

Time: 15 minutes | Serves 2

Ingredients:

- 1-pound fresh spinach, washed and drained
- 2 garlic clove, thinly sliced
- ½ cup raisins

- ½ cup pine nuts
- 2 tablespoons olive oil
- Salt and black pepper to taste
- A splash of red wine vinegar or sherry vinegar

Method:

1. In a large skillet, heat the olive oil over medium heat.
2. Add the garlic, raisins, and pine nuts. Sauté for 2-3 minutes until the garlic is golden and the pine nuts are toasted.
3. Gradually add the spinach to the skillet, tossing constantly until it begins to wilt. Depending on the size of your skillet, you may need to add the spinach in batches.
4. Once all the spinach has wilted, season with salt and pepper. Stir well to combine all the ingredients.
5. Drizzle with a splash of vinegar, and toss again to distribute the vinegar evenly. Serve immediately.

Per Serving:

Calories: 211, Fat: 15g, Carbs: 25g, Protein: 8g

90.   Simple Sautéed Cauliflower

Time: 10 minutes | Serves 2

Ingredients:

- Salt and freshly ground black pepper, to taste
- 1 medium head cauliflower, cut into florets
- 2 tablespoons olive oil

Optional:

- 2 garlic cloves, minced
- A pinch of red pepper flakes

Method:

1. Heat the olive oil in a large skillet over medium heat.
2. Add the cauliflower florets to the skillet. If using garlic or red pepper flakes, add them now.
3. Sauté the cauliflower for about 8-10 minutes, stirring occasionally, until the florets are golden brown and tender.
4. Season with salt and freshly ground black pepper. Serve immediately.

Per Serving:

Calories: 116.5; Fat: 9g; Carbs: 8g; Protein: 3.7g

91.   Feta and Cheese Couscous

Time: 10 minutes | Serves 2

Ingredients:

- 1 cup couscous
- 1 ¼ cup water or vegetable broth
- ½ cup crumbled feta cheese
- ¼ cup grated Parmesan cheese
- 2 tablespoons olive oil
- Salt and black pepper, to taste

Optional:

- ¼ cup chopped fresh parsley
- Basil, to taste

Method:

1. Bring the water or vegetable broth to a boil in a medium saucepan.
2. Add the couscous to the boiling water or broth, stir once, and then cover the saucepan. Remove from heat and let it stand for 5 minutes, or until the liquid is absorbed and the couscous is tender.
3. Fluff the couscous gently with a fork to separate the grains.
4. Stir in the olive oil, feta cheese, and Parmesan cheese until well combined. Season with salt and freshly ground black pepper to taste.

5. If desired, mix in chopped parsley or basil for added flavor and color.
6. Serve warm as a side dish or as part of a main meal.

Per Serving:

Calories: 377; Fat: 14.3g; Carbs: 34.5g; Protein: 16.2g

92.   Vegetable Cakes

Time: 10 minutes | Serves 2

Ingredients:

- 1 cup zucchini, grated
- ½ cup potato, grated
- 1 cup carrots, grated
- 1 small onion, finely chopped
- 2 garlic cloves, minced
- ¼ cup all-purpose flour
- 2 large eggs beaten
- 2 tablespoons olive oil, for frying
- ¼ teaspoon freshly ground black pepper
- ½ teaspoon salt

Method:

1. Place the grated zucchini, carrots, and potato in a clean kitchen towel and squeeze out as much excess liquid as possible.
2. In a large bowl, combine the squeezed vegetables, onion, garlic, flour, and eggs. Stir until well combined. Season with salt and pepper.
3. Heat the olive oil in a large skillet over medium heat. Form the vegetable mixture into small patties, about 3 inches in diameter.
4. Fry the patties in the hot oil, in batches if necessary, for about 4-5 minutes on each side or until golden brown and cooked through.
5. Transfer the vegetable cakes to a paper towel-lined plate to drain any excess oil. Serve warm.

Per Serving:

Calories: 223; Fat: 15g; Carbs: 25g; Protein: 7.1 g

93.   Grilled Eggplant with Basil and Parsley

Time: 10 minutes | Serves 2

Ingredients:

- 1 large eggplant, sliced into ½ inch thick rounds
- 2 tablespoons olive oil
- ¼ cup fresh parsley leaves, finely chopped
- ¼ cup fresh basil leaves, finely chopped
- Salt and freshly ground black pepper, to taste

Optional:

- Lemon juice
- balsamic glaze for drizzling

Method:

1. Preheat a grill or grill pan over medium-high heat.
2. Brush both sides of the eggplant slices with olive oil and season with salt and pepper.
3. Grill the eggplant slices for about 4-5 minutes on each side, or until tender and grill marks appear.
4. Once grilled, transfer the eggplant slices to a serving platter. Sprinkle the chopped basil and parsley over the warm eggplant.
5. If desired, drizzle with balsamic glaze or a squeeze of lemon juice for added flavor. Serve immediately.

Per Serving

Calories: 163; Fat: 15g; Carbs: 8.4g; Protein: 2g

94. Orzo with Herbs

Time: 15 minutes | Serves 2

Ingredients:

- 1 cup orzo pasta
- 2 tablespoons olive oil
- ¼ cup chopped fresh herbs (such as basil, thyme or parsley)
- Salt and pepper, to taste

Optional:

- zest of 1 lemon for freshness
- ¼ cup grated Parmesan cheese

Method:

1. Bring a large pot of salted water to a boil. Add the orzo and cook according to package instructions until al dente, usually about 7-9 minutes.
2. Drain the orzo and return it to the pot.
3. Stir in the olive oil, chopped herbs, and lemon zest if using. Mix until the orzo is well coated with the herbs and oil.
4. Season with salt and freshly ground black pepper to taste.
5. If desired, stir in the grated Parmesan cheese for extra flavor and richness. Serve warm.

Per Serving:

Calories: 260; Fat: 14g; Carbs: 40g; Protein: 7g

95. Basil Artichoke

Time: 15 minutes | Serves 2

Ingredients:

- 2 garlic cloves, minced
- Salt and black pepper, to taste

- 1 can artichoke hearts, drained and quartered
- 2 tablespoons olive oil
- ¼ cup fresh basil leaves, chopped

Method:

1. Heat the olive oil in a skillet over medium heat.
2. Add the minced garlic to the skillet and sauté for about 1 minute, or until fragrant.
3. Add the artichoke hearts to the skillet and sauté for about 3-4 minutes, or until they are heated through and slightly golden.
4. Stir in the chopped basil, and season with salt and freshly ground black pepper. Cook for an additional minute to allow the flavors to meld.
5. Serve warm as a side dish or incorporate into salads.

Per Serving:

Calories: 40; Fat: 3.4; Carbs: 1.8g; Protein: 0.5g

96.　Chili Broccoli

Time: 15 minutes | Serves 2

Ingredients:

- 1 large head of broccoli, cut into florets
- 1 teaspoon chili flakes
- 2 tablespoons olive oil
- Salt, to taste

Method:

1. Bring a large pot of water to a boil. Blanch the broccoli florets for about 2 minutes, just until they start to become tender but still retain their crispness.
2. Drain the broccoli and immediately rinse under cold water to stop the cooking process.
3. Heat the olive oil in a large skillet over medium heat. If using garlic, add it to the skillet and sauté until fragrant, about 1 minute.

4. Add the blanched broccoli florets to the skillet. Sprinkle with chili flakes and salt.
5. Sauté for about 5-7 minutes, stirring occasionally, until the broccoli is heated through and starts to char slightly on the edges. Serve immediately.

Per Serving

Calories: 158; Fat: 8g; Carbs: 12g; Protein: 4g

97.   Cauliflower Rice

Time: 15 minutes | Serves 2

Ingredients:

- 1 medium cauliflower, trimmed and cut into chunks
- 2 tablespoons olive oil
- Salt and pepper, to taste

Optional:

- 2 garlic cloves, minced
- ½ teaspoon of your favorite herbs

Method:

1. Place the cauliflower chunks in a food processor and pulse until the cauliflower resembles the texture of rice. Be careful not to over-process to avoid making it mushy.
2. Heat the olive oil in a large skillet over medium heat. If using garlic, add it to the skillet and sauté until fragrant, about 1 minute.
3. Add the cauliflower rice to the skillet. Season with salt and black pepper.
4. Stir-fry for about 5-8 minutes, or until the cauliflower is tender and slightly crispy.
5. If using, sprinkle with your chosen herbs just before serving.
6. Serve warm as a side dish or use as a base for dishes that typically use rice.

Per Serving:

Calories: 113; Fat: 6g; Carbs: 15g; Protein: 5g

98.   Veggie Rice Bowls with Pesto Sauce

Time: 15 minutes | Serves 2

Ingredients:

- 2 cups water
- 1 cup arborio rice, rinsed
- Salt and ground black pepper, to taste
- 2 eggs
- 1 cup broccoli florets
- ½ pound Brussels sprouts
- 1 carrot, peeled and chopped
- 1 small beet, peeled and cubed
- ¼ cup pesto sauce
- Lemon wedges, for serving

Method:

1. Combine the water, rice, salt, and pepper in the Instant Pot. Insert a trivet over rice and place a steamer basket on top.
2. Add the eggs, broccoli, Brussels sprouts, carrots, beet cubes, salt, and pepper to the steamer basket. Lock the lid. Select the Manual mode and set the cooking time for 1 minute at High Pressure.
3. When the timer beeps, perform a natural pressure release for 10 minutes, then release any remaining pressure. Carefully open the lid.
4. Remove the steamer basket and trivet from the pot and transfer the eggs to a bowl of ice water. Peel and halve the eggs. Use a fork to fluff the rice.
5. Divide the rice, broccoli, Brussels sprouts, carrot, beet cubes, and eggs into two bowls.
6. Top with a dollop of pesto sauce and serve with the lemon wedges.

Per Serving:

Calories: 590, Fat: 34.1g, Carbs: 50.0g, Protein: 21.9g

99.   Sautéed Spinach and Leeks

Time: 13 minutes | Serves 2

Ingredients:

- 3 tablespoons olive oil
- 2 garlic cloves, crushed
- 2 leeks, chopped
- 2 red onions, chopped
- 9 ounces' fresh spinach
- 1 teaspoon kosher salt
- ½ cup crumbled goat cheese

Method:

1. Coat the bottom of the Instant Pot with the olive oil.
2. Add the garlic, leek, and onions and stir-fry for about 5 minutes, on Sauté mode.
3. Stir in the spinach. Sprinkle with the salt and sauté for an additional 3 minutes, stirring constantly.
4. Transfer to a plate and scatter with the goat cheese before serving.

Per Serving

Calories: 447 Fat: 31.2g Protein: 14.6g Carbs: 28.7g

100.   Simple Honey-Glazed Baby Carrots

Time: 11 minutes | Serves 2

Ingredients:

- ⅔ cup water
- 1½ pounds baby carrots
- 4 tablespoons almond butter

- ½ cup honey
- 1 teaspoon dried thyme
- 1½ teaspoons dried dill
- Salt, to taste

Method:

1. Pour the water into the Instant Pot and add a steamer basket. Place the baby carrots in the basket. Secure the lid.
2. Select the Manual mode and set the cooking time for 4 minutes at High Pressure.
3. Once cooking is complete, do a quick pressure release. Carefully open the lid. Transfer the carrots to a plate and set aside.
4. Pour the water out of the Instant Pot and dry it. Press the Sauté button on the Instant Pot and heat the almond butter.
5. Stir in the honey, thyme, and dill. Return the carrots to the Instant Pot and stir until well coated. Sauté for another 1 minute.
6. Taste and season with salt as needed. Serve warm.

Per Serving

Calories: 575, Fat: 23.5g, Carbs: 90.6g, Protein: 2.8g

Poultry

101.   Chicken Bruschetta Burgers

Time: 15 minutes | Serves 2

Ingredients:

- 1 tablespoon olive oil
- 2 garlic cloves, minced
- 3 tablespoons finely minced onion
- 1 teaspoon dried basil
- 3 tablespoons minced sun-dried tomatoes packed in olive oil
- 8 ounces ground chicken breast
- ¼ teaspoon salt
- 3 pieces small Mozzarella balls, minced

Method:

1. Heat the olive oil in a nonstick skillet over medium-high heat. Add the garlic and onion and sauté for 5 minutes until tender. Stir in the basil.
2. Remove from the skillet to a medium bowl.
3. Add the tomatoes, ground chicken, and salt and stir until incorporated. Mix in the Mozzarella balls.
4. Divide the chicken mixture in half and form into two burgers, each about ¾-inch thick.
5. Heat the same skillet over medium-high heat and add the burgers.
6. Cook each side for 5 to 6 minutes, or until they reach an internal temperature of 165°F. Serve warm.

Per Serving

Calories: 300, Fat: 17.0g, Carbs: 6.0g, Protein: 32.2g

102. Chicken Gyros with Tzatziki Sauce

Time: 10 minutes | Serves 2

Ingredients:

- 2 tablespoons freshly squeezed lemon juice
- 2 tablespoons olive oil, divided, plus more for oiling the grill
- 1 teaspoon minced fresh oregano
- ½ teaspoon garlic powder
- Salt, to taste
- 8 ounces' chicken tenders
- 1 small eggplant, cut into 1-inch strips lengthwise
- 1 small zucchini, cut into ½-inch strips lengthwise
- ½ red pepper, seeded and cut in half lengthwise
- ½ English cucumber, peeled and minced
- ¾ cup plain Greek yogurt
- 1 tablespoon minced fresh dill
- 2 (8-inch) pita breads

Method:

1. Combine the lemon juice, 1 tablespoon of olive oil, oregano, garlic powder, and salt in a medium bowl. Add the chicken and let marinate for 30 minutes.
2. Place the eggplant, zucchini, and red pepper in a large mixing bowl and sprinkle with salt and the remaining 1 tablespoon of olive oil. Toss well to coat. Let the vegetables rest while the chicken is marinating.
3. Combine the cucumber, yogurt, salt, and dill in a medium bowl. Stir well to incorporate and set aside in the refrigerator.
4. When ready, preheat the grill to medium-high heat and oil the grill grates. Drain any liquid from the vegetables and put them on the grill. Remove the chicken tenders from the marinade and put them on the grill.
5. Grill the chicken and vegetables for 3 minutes per side, or until the chicken is no longer pink inside. Remove the chicken and vegetables from the grill and set aside.
6. On the grill, heat the pitas for about 30 seconds, flipping them frequently.

7. Divide the chicken tenders and vegetables between the pitas and top each with ¼ cup of the prepared sauce. Roll the pitas up like a cone and serve.

Per Serving

Calories: 586, Fat: 21.9g, Carbs: 62.0g, Protein: 39.0g

103.   Sicilian Olive Chicken

Time: 15 minutes | Serves 2

Ingredients:

- chicken cutlets, each about 4-ounce
- ¼ teaspoon crushed red pepper
- 7-ounce cherry tomatoes halved
- ½ tablespoon capers, rinsed
- ¼ cup Sicilian olive halves
- ¼ teaspoon ground black pepper
- ¾ cup chopped spinach, thawed if frozen
- ½ tablespoon olive oil

Method:

1. Take a large bowl, place tomatoes, olive, spinach, capers and red pepper. Stir until well mixed.
2. Place the chicken cutlets on a cutting board, and then season with black pepper until coated.
3. Take a medium skillet pan, place it over medium-high heat, add oil, and when hot, add the prepared chicken cutlets and then cook for 4 to 5 minutes per side until nicely brown.
4. Add the prepared tomato mixture to the pan, switch heat to medium level, cover the pan with its lid and then cook for 5 minutes until the chicken has thoroughly cooked.
5. When done, place the chicken on a serving plate, add the tomato mixture on the side, and serve.

Calories: 213; Fat: 8.4g; Carbs: 9.3g; Protein: 26.1g

104.   Chicken Skillet with Mushrooms

Time: 15 minutes | Serves 2

Ingredients:

- 5-ounce Portobello mushrooms, sliced
- ½ of a large white onion, peeled, cut into round slices
- 1-pound chicken breast, cut into strips
- ¼ teaspoon salt, divided
- ¼ teaspoon ground black pepper, divided
- ½ teaspoon dried thyme
- 1 ½ tablespoon olive oil, divided
- ½ tablespoon balsamic vinegar
- 3 tablespoons white wine
- ¼ cup vegetable broth
- 1-ounce parmesan cheese, sliced

Method:

1. Take a large bowl, place chicken strips in it, add salt, black pepper, and thyme, pour in oil, vinegar, and white wine, toss until well coated, and set aside until required.
2. Take a medium skillet pan, place it over medium heat, add oil, and when hot, add onion and cook for 1 minute until begin to tender.
3. Add mushroom, salt, and black pepper, pour in the vegetable broth, cook for 5 minutes until softened, and when done, transfer the mushroom mixture into a bowl.
4. Then add marinated chicken into the pan, cook for 5 minutes, return the mushroom mixture into the pan, and cook for 3 minutes until thoroughly hot.
5. When done, place the cooked mushroom chicken into a serving plate, place parmesan slices on the side, and serve.

105.   Grilled Chicken Breasts with Spinach Pesto

Time: 15 minutes | Serves 2

Ingredients:

- 2 boneless, skinless chicken breasts
- ¼ cup + 1 tbsp. olive oil
- ½ cup spinach
- ¼ cup grated Pecorino cheese
- Salt and black pepper to taste
- ¼ cup pine nuts
- 1 garlic clove, minced

Method:

1. Rub chicken with salt and black pepper.
2. Grease a grill pan with 1 tbsp. of olive oil and place over medium heat.
3. Grill the chicken for 8-10 minutes, flipping once. Mix spinach, garlic, Pecorino cheese, and pine nuts in a food processor.
4. Slowly, pour in the remaining oil; pulse until smooth.
5. Spoon 1 tbsp. of pesto on each breast and cook for an additional 5 minutes.

Per Serving:

Calories: 493, Fat: 27g, Carbs: 4g, Protein: 53g

106.   Vegetable & Chicken Skewers

Time: 15 minutes | Serves 2

Ingredients:

- 2 tbsp. olive oil
- 1 chicken breast, cubed
- ½ red bell pepper, cut into squares
- ½ red onion, cut into squares
- ½ cup mushrooms, quartered
- 1 tsp sweet paprika
- 1 tsp ground nutmeg
- 1 tsp Italian seasoning
- ¼ tsp smoked paprika
- Salt and black pepper to taste
- ¼ tsp ground cardamom
- 1 lemon, juiced
- 2 garlic cloves, minced

Method:

1. Combine chicken, onion, bell pepper, paprika, nutmeg, Italian seasoning, paprika, salt, pepper, cardamom, lemon juice, garlic, and olive oil in a bowl.
2. Transfer to the fridge covered for 30 minutes.
3. Preheat your grill to high. Alternate chicken cubes, peppers, mushrooms, and onions on each of 4 metal skewers.
4. Grill them for 16 minutes on all sides, turning frequently. Serve with salad.

Per Serving:

Calories: 270, Fat: 15g, Carbs: 15g, Protein: 21g

107.   Tuscan Style Chicken

Time: 10 minutes | Serves 2

Ingredients:

- 5 oz. chicken breast, skinless, boneless, roughly chopped
- 1 tablespoon olive oil
- ½ cup organic almond milk
- 1 oz. Parmesan, grated

- ½ teaspoon chili flakes
- ¼ teaspoon ground nutmeg

Method:

1. Heat the olive oil, add chicken breast, and sprinkle with chili flakes.
2. Roast the chicken for 3 minutes and stir.
3. Then add almond milk, ground nutmeg, and Parmesan.
4. Close the lid and simmer the chicken for 20 minutes on low heat.

Per Serving

Calories: 270; Fat: 13g; Carbs: 20g; Protein: 17g

108.　　Turkey with Rigatoni

Time: 14 minutes | Serves 2

Ingredients:

- 2 tbsp. canola oil
- ½ pound ground turkey
- 1 egg
- ¼ cup bread crumbs
- 1 clove garlic, minced
- 1 tsp dried oregano
- Salt and ground black pepper to taste
- 1 cup tomato sauce
- ounces rigatoni
- 2 tbsp. grated Grana Padano cheese

Method:

1. In a bowl, combine turkey, crumbs, cumin, garlic, and egg. Season with oregano, salt, red pepper flakes, and pepper.
2. Form the mixture into meatballs with well-oiled hands.
3. Warm the oil on Sauté. Cook the meatballs for 3 to 4 minutes, until browned on all sides. Remove to a plate.

4. Add rigatoni to the cooker and cover with tomato sauce.
5. Pour enough water to cover the pasta. Stir well. Throw in the meatballs.
6. Seal the lid and cook for 10 minutes on High Pressure. Release the Pressure quickly. Serve topped with Grana Padano cheese.

Per Serving:

Calories 470, Fat 10g, Carbs 61g, Protein 33g

109.   Greek Turkey Meatballs

Time: 10 minutes | Serves 2

Ingredients:

- 1 onion, minced
- ½ cup plain bread crumbs
- ⅓ cup feta cheese, crumbled
- 1 tsp salt
- ½ tsp dried oregano
- ¼ tsp ground black pepper
- ½ pound ground turkey
- 1 egg, lightly beaten
- 1 tbsp. olive oil
- 1 carrot, minced
- ½ celery stalk, minced
- 1 cups tomato puree
- 2 cups water

Method:

1. In a mixing bowl, combine half the onion, oregano, turkey, salt, crumbs, pepper, and egg, and stir until everything is well incorporated.
2. Heat oil on Sauté mode, and cook celery, remaining onion, and carrot for 5 minutes, until soft. Pour in water, and tomato puree. Adjust the seasonings.
3. Roll the mixture into meatballs, and drop into the sauce. Seal the lid.
4. Press Meat Stew and cook on High Pressure for 5 minutes.

5. Allow the cooker to cool and release the pressure naturally for 20 minutes. Serve topped with feta cheese.

Per Serving:

Calories 214.7, Fat 10.5g, Carbs 10.3g, Protein 19.6g

110.   Turkey Patties

Time: 15 minutes | Serves 2

Ingredients:

- ½ lb. ground turkey
- 1 egg
- ½ cup flour

- 1 onion, finely chopped
- 2 tsp dried dill, chopped
- ½ tsp salt
- ½ tsp black pepper, ground
- ½ cup sour cream

Method:

1. In a bowl, add all Ingredients: and mix well with hands.
2. Form the patties with the previously prepared mixture. Line parchment paper over a baking dish and arrange the patties.
3. Pour 1 cup of water in the pot. Lay the trivet and place the baking dish on top.
4. Seal the lid. Cook on Pressure Cook mode for 15 minutes on High. Release the pressure naturally, for 10 minutes.
5. Serve with lettuce and tomatoes.

Per Serving:

Calories 251, Fat 14.4g, Carbs 6.2g, Protein 22.9g

111. Hot Chicken with Black Beans

Time: 15 minutes | Serves 2

Ingredients:

- ½ cup chicken broth
- 1 tbsp. honey
- 2 tbsp. tomato paste
- ½ cup hot sauce
- 1 garlic clove, grated
- 2 boneless, skinless chicken drumsticks
- 1 tbsp. cornstarch
- 1 tbsp. water
- 1 tbsp. olive oil
- 1 cup canned black beans
- 1 green onion, thinly chopped

Method:

1. In the cooker, mix the hot sauce, honey, tomato paste, chicken broth, and garlic.
2. Stir well until smooth; toss in the chicken to coat.
3. Seal the lid and cook for 3 minutes on High Pressure. Release the Pressure immediately.
4. Open the lid and press Sauté. In a small bowl, mix water and cornstarch until no lumps remain, Stir into the sauce and cook for 5 minutes until thickened.
5. Stir in olive oil and black beans; garnish with green onions and serve.

Per Serving:

Calories 307.3, Fat 2.9g, Carbs 40.0g, Protein 30.5g

112. Turkey Pepperoni Pizza

Time: 15 minutes | Serves 2

Ingredients:

- ½ wheat Italian pizza crust
- 1 cup fire-roasted tomatoes, diced
- 1 tsp oregano
- ½ tsp dried basil
- ½ cup turkey pepperoni, chopped
- 3 oz. Gouda cheese, grated
- 2 tbsp. olive oil

Method:

1. Grease a baking pan with oil. Line some parchment paper and place the pizza crust in it.
2. Spread the fire-roasted tomatoes over the pizza crust and sprinkle with oregano and basil.
3. Make a layer with cheese and Top with pepperoni.
4. Add a trivet inside the pot and pour in 1 cup of water. Seal the lid, and cook for 15 minutes on High Pressure.
5. Do a quick release. Remove the pizza from the pot using a parchment paper.

Per Serving:

Calories 216, Fat 7.7g, Carbs 22.3g, Protein 14g

113. Bruschetta Chicken Burgers

Time: 15 minutes | Serves 2

Ingredients:

- 1 tablespoon olive oil
- 3 tablespoons finely minced onion
- 2 garlic cloves, minced
- 1 teaspoon dried basil
- ¼ teaspoon salt
- 3 tablespoons minced sun-dried tomatoes packed in olive oil

- 8 ounces ground chicken breast
- 3 pieces' small mozzarella balls (ciliegine), minced

Method:

1. Heat the grill to high heat (about 400°F) and oil the grill grates. Alternatively, you can cook these in a nonstick skillet.
2. Heat the olive oil in a small skillet over medium-high heat. Add the onion and garlic and sauté for 5 minutes, until softened. Stir in the basil. Remove from the heat and place in a medium bowl.
3. Add the salt, sun-dried tomatoes, and ground chicken and stir to combine. Mix in the mozzarella balls.
4. Divide the chicken mixture in half and form into two burgers, each about ¾-inch thick.
5. Place the burgers on the grill and cook for five minutes, or until golden on the bottom. Flip the burgers over and grill for another five minutes, or until they reach an internal temperature of 165°F.
6. If cooking the burgers in a skillet on the stovetop, heat a nonstick skillet over medium-high heat and add the burgers. Cook them for 5 to 6 minutes on the first side, or until golden brown on the bottom. Flip the burgers and cook for an additional 5 minutes, or until they reach an internal temperature of 165°F.

Per Serving:

Calories: 301; fat: 17g; carbs: 6g; Protein: 32g

114.   Lemony Turkey and Pine Nuts

Time: 15 minutes | Serves 2

Ingredients:

- ½ pound ground turkey
- ¼ teaspoon black pepper
- 2 tablespoon pine nuts
- Juice of ½ lemon
- Zest of 1 lemon

- 1 garlic clove, minced
- ¼ teaspoon salt
- 1 small onion, finely chopped
- 1 tablespoon olive oil
- 2 tablespoons fresh parsley, chopped

Method:

1. In a dry skillet, toast the pine nuts over medium heat until golden and fragrant, about 3-4 minutes.
2. Remove from the skillet and set aside. In the same skillet, heat the olive oil over medium heat.
3. Add the chopped onion and cook until softened, about 5 minutes. Add the minced garlic and cook for an additional minute until fragrant.
4. Add the ground turkey to the skillet. Cook, breaking it up with a spoon, until the turkey is browned and cooked through, about 7-8 minutes.
5. Stir in the lemon zest, lemon juice, toasted pine nuts, salt and pepper.
6. Remove from heat and stir in the chopped parsley. Serve the turkey mixture warm.

Per Serving:

Calories: 293, fat: 12.4g, carbs: 7.8g, protein 34g

115.   Lemon and Paprika Herb-Marinated Chicken

Time: 15 minutes | Serves 2

Ingredients:

- 2 tablespoons olive oil
- 4 tablespoons freshly squeezed lemon juice
- ¼ teaspoon salt 1 teaspoon paprika
- 1 teaspoon dried basil
- ½ teaspoon dried thyme
- ¼ teaspoon garlic powder
- 2 (4-ounce) boneless, skinless chicken breasts

Method:

1. In a bowl with a lid, combine the olive oil, lemon juice, salt, paprika, basil, thyme, and garlic powder.
2. Add the chicken and marinate for at least 30 minutes, or up to 4 hours.
3. When ready to cook, heat the grill to medium-high (about 350–400°F) and oil the grill grate. Alternately, you can also cook these in a nonstick sauté pan over medium-high heat.
4. Grill the chicken for 6 to 7 minutes, or until it lifts away from the grill easily. Flip it over and grill for another 6 to 7 minutes, or until it reaches an internal temperature of 165°F.

Per Serving:

Calories: 252; Fat: 16g; Carbs: 2g; Protein: 27g

116.   Mediterranean Chicken Salad Wraps

Time: 15 minutes | Serves 2

Ingredients:

For the tzatziki sauce

- ½ cup plain Greek yogurt
- 1 tablespoon freshly squeezed lemon juice
- 1 teaspoon dried dill
- Pinch garlic powder
- Salt Freshly ground black pepper

For the salad wraps

- 2 (8-inch) pita or naan bread
- 1 cup shredded chicken meat
- 2 cups mixed greens
- 2 roasted red bell peppers, sliced thin
- ½ English cucumber, peeled if desired and sliced thin
- ¼ cup pitted black olives

- 1 scallion, chopped

Method:

1. Combine the Greek yogurt, lemon juice, dill, and garlic powder in a small bowl and season with salt and pepper.
2. On each piece of pita or naan bread, spread ¼ cup of the tzatziki sauce and arrange half the chicken, mixed greens, red pepper slices, cucumber, olives, and scallion.
3. Roll up the sandwiches and, if desired, wrap the bottom half of each sandwich in foil so it's easier to eat.

Per Serving:

Calories: 429; Fat: 11g; Carbs: 51g; Protein: 31g

117.   Spiced Chicken Thighs with Saffron Basmati Rice

Time: 15 minutes | Serves 2

Ingredients:

For the chicken

- ½ teaspoon paprika
- ½ teaspoon cumin
- ½ teaspoon cinnamon
- ¼ teaspoon salt
- ¼ teaspoon garlic powder
- ¼ teaspoon ginger powder
- ¼ teaspoon coriander
- ⅛ teaspoon cayenne pepper (a pinch—or more if you like it spicy)
- 10 ounces boneless, skinless chicken thighs (about 4 pieces)

For the rice

- 1 tablespoon olive oil

- ½ small onion, minced
- ½ cup basmati rice
- 2 pinches saffron
- ¼ teaspoon salt
- 1 cup low-sodium chicken stock

Method:

1. Preheat the oven to 350°F and set the rack to the middle position.
2. In a small bowl, combine the paprika, cumin, cinnamon, salt, garlic powder, ginger powder, coriander, and cayenne pepper. Add chicken thighs and toss, rubbing the spice mix into the chicken.
3. Place the chicken in a baking dish and roast it for 35 to 40 minutes, or until the chicken reaches an internal temperature of 165°F. Let the chicken rest for 5 minutes before serving.
4. While the chicken is roasting, heat the oil in a sauté pan over medium-high heat. Add the onion and sauté for 5 minutes.
5. Add the rice, saffron, salt, and chicken stock. Cover the pot with a tight-fitting lid and reduce the heat to low. Let the rice simmer for 15 minutes, or until it is light and fluffy and the liquid has been absorbed.

Per Serving:

Calories: 401; Fat: 10g; Carbs: 41g; Protein: 37g

118.   Chicken Souvlaki

Time: 15 minutes | Serves 2

Ingredients:

- 2 (boneless, skinless) chicken breasts, diced into cubes
- 2 tablespoons olive oil
- Juice from ½ lemon
- 1 garlic clove, minced
- 1 tablespoon dried oregano
- Salt and pepper, to taste

For the tzatziki

- 1 cucumber, peeled, seeded, and diced into small cubes
- 1 garlic clove, minced
- 2 tablespoons olive oil
- 10 ounces' Greek yogurt
- 1 tablespoon red wine vinegar
- Kosher salt, to taste

Method:

1. Place the diced chicken breasts in a large mixing bowl. To the bowl, add the olive oil, lemon juice, garlic, and oregano. Season with salt and pepper.
2. Cover the bowl with plastic wrap. Let the chicken marinate in the fridge for at least 30 minutes.
3. In the meantime, make the tzatziki. In a medium mixing bowl, combine the cucumber, garlic, olive oil, vinegar, and Greek yogurt. Season with more salt if desired.
4. Soak 4 wooden skewers in water. Insert the chicken cubes onto the skewers.
5. Heat a grill pan over medium heat, drizzling with some olive oil to prevent the chicken from sticking.
6. Cook the chicken skewers on each side until grilled, about 10-15 minutes' total. Serve the souvlaki with the tzatziki.

Per Serving:

Calories 542, Fat 28g, Carbs 14g, Protein 58g

119.   One-Pot Chicken Pesto Pasta

Time: 15 minutes | Serves 2

Ingredients:

- 8 ounces' whole-wheat penne
- ½ pound asparagus, trimmed and diced
- 2 cups cooked chicken or leftover shredded chicken

- 4 ounces' pesto
- Salt and pepper, to taste
- 2 tablespoons grated parmesan cheese

Method:

1. Bring a large pot of salted water to a boil.
2. Add the penne and cook per package directions.
3. Just 2 minutes before the pasta is done, add the asparagus.
4. Drain the pasta and asparagus.
5. In a large mixing bowl, combine the pasta, asparagus, chicken, pesto, parmesan cheese, salt and pepper. Serve warm.

Per Serving:

Calories 671, Fat 9g, Carbs 86g, Protein 67g

120. Greek Turkey Cutlets

Time: 12 minutes | Serves 2 (6 meatballs)

Ingredients:

- ½ lb. ground turkey/chicken
- ½ cup fresh spinach, chopped/broccoli/fresh greens
- 2 oz. feta/mozzarella, shredded
- ½ cup bell pepper, finely chopped
- ½ yellow onion, finely chopped
- 1 garlic clove, minced
- 1 whole egg, slightly beaten
- 2 Tbsp. breadcrumbs
- Salt, to taste
- 2 Tbsp. olive oil, for frying

Method:

1. Mix all the ingredients in a bowl.
2. Form small patties from the mixture using your hands.

3. Preheat olive oil in the skillet.
4. Fry patties for 8–12 minutes until golden brown, flipping them once.
5. Serve warm with seasonal salad, mashed potato, and sauce of your choice.

Per Serving:

Calories: 161, Carbs: 3.6g, Fat: 10.9g, Protein: 12.5g

Meats

121.   Sausages with Vegetables

Time: 15 minutes | Serves 2

Ingredients:

- 6 oz. pre-cooked sausage (Italian/Cajun/Andouille), diced
- ½ bell pepper, diced
- ½ white onion, diced
- ½ zucchini, diced
- 1 cup corn kernels (optional)
- ½ cup chicken broth
- 1 Tbsp. olive oil
- ¼ tsp. smoked paprika
- 1 Tbsp. spring onion, chopped

Method:

1. Heat olive oil in a frying pan over medium heat.
2. Add diced sausages and cook for 6 minutes until golden brown, flipping once. Remove the sausages from the pan and set aside.
3. Add diced vegetables to the pan and cook for 5 minutes, stirring occasionally.
4. Return sausages to the pan and stir in. Add smoked paprika and chicken broth, and cook for 5 minutes, stirring once.
5. Sprinkle with chopped spring onion and serve with pasta, rice, or crispy Italian bread.

Per Serving:

Calories: 467, Fat 30 g, Carbs: 30 g, Protein 22.1 g

122.   Kofta Kebabs

Time: 12 minutes | Serves 2

Ingredients:

- ½ lb. ground beef/lamb
- 1 garlic clove, minced
- 1 small red onion, finely chopped
- ¼ tsp. nutmeg
- ¼ tsp. allspice
- ¼ tsp. paprika
- ⅛ tsp. ground black pepper
- ¼ tsp. cumin
- ¼ tsp. cardamom
- ¼ tsp. sea salt

Method:

1. Mix all the ingredients in a food processor.
2. Shape 4 oval koftas using your hand. If you prefer, you can string the meat on skewers.
3. Arrange the koftas on a grill or in an air fryer basket in a single layer.
4. Cook at 350°F for 12 minutes until golden brown, flipping once.
5. Serve kofta kebabs with pita bread and grilled vegetables.
6. They perfectly pair with tahini sauce/baba ganoush/tzatziki sauce/hummus.

Per Serving:

Calories: 161, Fat: 4.6 g, Carbs: 4 g, Protein: 23.1 g

123.   Pork Chops in Wine Sauce

Time: 15 minutes | Serves 2

Ingredients:

- 2 pork chops (¾-inch thick), bone-in (at room temperature)
- 2 garlic cloves, crushed
- 1 garlic clove, diced
- 8 oz. button mushrooms, diced

- ½ cup dry red wine
- ½ cup (120 ml) water
- 10 sprigs of thyme/rosemary
- 2 Tbsp. unsalted butter
- 1 Tbsp. olive oil
- Salt and pepper, to taste

Method:

1. Pat the pork chops dry and rub with crushed garlic, salt, and pepper.
2. Heat olive oil in a frying pan over medium heat. Add garlic and thyme sprigs and cook for 1–2 minutes, stirring occasionally.
3. Add 1 tablespoon of butter and diced mushrooms. Cook for 4–5 minutes until golden. Remove mushrooms, thyme, and garlic from the pan and set aside.
4. Melt the remaining butter in the pan and add pork chops. Cook for 2 minutes on each side until golden.
5. Return mushrooms and garlic to the pan. Add red wine and water. Simmer for 5 minutes, flipping the chops once.
6. Remove from the heat, cover with a lid, and let stand for 5–7 minutes.
7. Serve with roasted potatoes and vegetables. Pour the pork chops with the wine-mushroom sauce from the pan.

Per Serving:

Calories 499, Fat 39 g, Carbs: 7.7 g, Protein 21 g

124.   Grilled Lamb Chops

Time: 15 minutes | Serves 2

Ingredients:

- 4 lamb chops (1 lb.), patted dry
- Garlic salted butter
- For the Marinade:
- 1 Tbsp. olive oil
- 1 Tbsp. Greek yogurt

- 1 garlic clove, minced
- 1 tsp. fresh rosemary
- ¼ tsp. black pepper
- 1 tsp. lemon juice
- ¼ tsp. lemon zest
- ¼ tsp. sea salt

Method:

1. Mix all the ingredients for the marinade in a bowl. Cover lamb chops with the marinade and let them stand.
2. Preheat your grill or frying pan. Cook for 7–9 minutes for medium-rare and 11–13 minutes for medium-well. Flip halfway through.
3. Drizzle with the remaining marinade every 3–4 minutes. Garnish with fresh rosemary sprigs and thyme.
4. Serve with fresh seasonal salad and arugula leaves.

Per Serving:

Calories: 409, Carbs: 0.7 g, Fat: 22.2 g, Protein: 50 g

125.   Pan-Seared Pork Chops

Time: 15 minutes | Serves 2

Ingredients:

Ingredients:

- 4 bone-in pork chops, approximately 1 inch thick
- 1 tablespoon olive oil
- 1 teaspoon salt
- ½ teaspoon black pepper
- ½ teaspoon garlic powder
- ½ teaspoon paprika

Optional:

- fresh herbs for garnish (such as thyme or rosemary)

Method

1. To create a flavorful blend, combine the salt, black pepper, garlic powder, and paprika in a small bowl, ensuring all ingredients are thoroughly mixed.
2. Ensure the pork chops are thoroughly dried by gently patting them with a paper towel. Then, generously season each side of the chops with the spice mixture, making sure to cover them evenly.
3. Start the cooking process by heating the olive oil in a large skillet over medium-high heat until it reaches the desired temperature.
4. After the oil has reached the desired temperature, proceed by placing the pork chops into the skillet. Let them cook for about 4-5 minutes on each side, or until the internal temperature reaches 145°F for a medium-rare doneness level, or 160°F for a medium doneness level.
5. Make sure to use a meat thermometer to accurately gauge the temperature. Remove the pork chops from the skillet and let them rest for a few minutes before serving.
6. Garnish with fresh herbs, such as thyme or rosemary, before serving. Serve the pan-seared pork chops hot, with your choice of side dishes.

Per Serving:

Calories: 250 Kcal, Fat: 15g, Carbs: 0g, Protein: 27g

126.   Hamburgers

Time: 10 minutes | Serves 2

Ingredients:

- 1-pound ground beef, extra-lean
- ¼ teaspoon garlic powder
- ¼ cup chopped roasted red bell pepper, divided
- ½ teaspoon salt
- ¼ cup sliced onion
- ¼ teaspoon ground black pepper

- ¼ cup arugula leaves, fresh
- ½ teaspoon ground cumin
- 2 tablespoons chopped parsley, fresh
- ¼ teaspoon ground oregano
- ¼ teaspoon paprika
- 2 whole-wheat hamburger buns
- 2 tablespoons crumbled feta cheese, low fat

Method

1. Take a griddle pan greased with oil, place it over medium-high heat and let it preheat.
2. Meanwhile, take a large bowl, add beef, bell pepper, cumin, oregano, paprika, garlic powder, black pepper, parsley, and salt, stir until well combined, and then shape the mixture into 2 patties.
3. Place the prepared patties on the griddle pan, and then cook for 5 minutes per side until thoroughly cooked and brown.
4. Then place hamburgers on the griddle pan, grill for a minute until hot and toasted, and place them on a plate.
5. Assemble the hamburger and for this, place bell pepper, onion, arugula, and feta cheese on the bottom slice of the bun and then top with the cooked patty.
6. Cover with the top side of the bun and then serve.

Per Serving

Calories: 270; Fat: 13g; Carbs: 20g; Protein: 17g

127.   Greek-Style Lamb Burgers

Time: 10 minutes | Serves 2

Ingredients:

- ½-pound ground lamb
- ½ teaspoon salt
- ½ teaspoon freshly ground black pepper
- 1 tablespoon crumbled feta cheese

- Buns, toppings, and tzatziki, for serving (optional)

Method

1. Preheat the grill to high heat. In a wide bowl, stir the lamb with salt and pepper using your hands.
2. Divide the meat into 2 portions. Divide each portion in half to make a top and a bottom. Flatten each half into a 3-inch circle.
3. Make a dent in the center of one of the halves and place 1 tablespoon of feta cheese in the center.
4. Place the second half of the patty on top of the feta cheese and press down to close the 2 halves together, making it resemble a round burger.
5. Grill each side for 3 minutes, for medium-well.
6. If desired, serve on a bun with your favorite toppings and tzatziki sauce.

Per Serving

Calories: 345; Fat: 29.0g; Carbs: 1.0g, Protein: 20.0g

128.   Easy Pork Chops in Tomato Sauce

Time: 10 minutes | Serves 2

Ingredients:

- 2 tbsp. olive oil
- 2 pork loin chops, boneless
- 3 tomatoes, peeled and crushed
- 2 tbsp. basil, chopped
- ¼ cup black olives pitted and halved
- ½ yellow onion, chopped
- 1 garlic clove, minced

Method

1. Warm the olive oil in a skillet over medium heat and brown pork chops for 6 minutes on all sides. Share into plates.

2. In the same skillet, stir tomatoes, basil, olives, onion, and garlic and simmer for 4 minutes.
3. Drizzle tomato sauce over pork to serve.

Per Serving:

Calories: 340, Fat: 18g, Carbs: 13g, Protein: 35g

129.   Fennel Lamb Chops

Time: 15 minutes | Serves 2

Ingredients:

- 4 lamb chops

- 3-ounce arugula leaves, fresh
- ½ medium fennel bulb, halved, sliced
- ¼ teaspoon salt, divided
- 1 tablespoon oregano leaves, fresh
- ½ teaspoon chopped garlic
- ¼ teaspoon ground black pepper, divided
- 2 medium tomatoes, sliced
- 3 teaspoons olive oil
- 2 teaspoons lemon juice

Method

1. Switch on the oven, set the temperature to 205 degrees C or 400 degrees F, and preheat.
2. Meanwhile, take a baking tray, line it with parchment paper, and set it aside until required.
3. Place the lamb chops on a cutting board and then season with salt and black pepper until coated.
4. Take a large skillet pan, place it over medium-high heat, add oil and when hot, place the lamb chops and then cook for 4 minutes per side or until golden.
5. Transfer the lamb chops onto the prepared baking tray and bake for 8 minutes

or thoroughly cooked.

6. Meanwhile, take a medium bowl, add tomatoes, oregano, garlic, fennel, lemon juice, oil, salt, and black pepper, and stir until combined.
7. When done, place the lamb chops on a serving plate, add arugula leaves on the side, and spoon the prepared tomato mixture over the arugula and serve.

Per Serving

Calories: 232; Fat: 12g; Carbs: 6.8g; Protein: 24.5g

130.   Lamb Meatballs with Tzatziki

Time: 15 minutes | Serves 2

Ingredients:

- ½ pound ground lamb
- ¼ teaspoon minced garlic
- ½ teaspoon salt
- 3 teaspoon pork rinds, blended
- 3 tablespoon chopped parsley, fresh
- 1 teaspoon ground cumin
- ¼ teaspoon ground black pepper
- ½ tablespoon chopped dill, fresh
- ½ teaspoon ground coriander
- 1 tablespoon olive oil
- ½ cup tzatziki sauce
- 1 large egg, at room temperature

Method

1. Switch on the oven, set the temperature to 205 degrees C or 400 degrees F, and preheat.
2. Meanwhile, take a baking tray, line it with parchment paper, and set it aside until required.
3. Take a large bowl, crack the egg in it, add lamb, pork rinds, parsley, oregano, cumin, coriander, garlic, black pepper, and salt, and stir until combined.

4. Shape the mixture into evenly sized meatballs, arrange them on the prepared baking tray and then bake for 20 minutes until thoroughly cooked.
5. When done, place the meatballs on a serving plate, and then serve with tzatziki sauce.

Per Serving

Calories: 212; Fat: 14.2g; Carbs: 2.8g; Protein: 18.3g

131.   Basil Meatballs

Time: 10 minutes | Serves 2

Ingredients:

- 5 oz ground pork

- 1 teaspoon dried basil
- ½ teaspoon chili flakes
- 2 tablespoons water
- 1 teaspoon ground paprika
- 1 tablespoon olive oil

Method

1. Mix ground pork with basil, chili flakes, water, and ground paprika.
2. After this, make the small meatballs.
3. Preheat the olive oil in the skillet.
4. Add the meatballs in the hot oil and roast for 4 minutes per side.

Per Serving:

Calories: 133; Fat: 6g; Carbs: 2.5g; Protein: 18.6g

132.   Thyme Pork Steak

Time: 10 minutes | Serves 2

Ingredients:

- 2 pork steaks
- 1 tablespoon dried thyme

- 1 tablespoon balsamic vinegar
- 1 tablespoon olive oil

Method

1. Rub the meat with dried thyme and brush with balsamic vinegar and olive oil.
2. Leave the meat to marinate.
3. After this, preheat the skillet until hot.
4. Put the steaks in the hot skillet and roast for 6 minutes per side.

Per Serving:

Calories: 285; Fat: 21g; Carbs: 0.9g; Protein: 21.9g

133.   Lamb Chops with Herb Butter

Time: 14 minutes | Serves 2

Ingredients:

- 3 lamb chops
- 1 tbsp. butter
- 1 tbsp. olive oil
- Salt
- Pepper
- 4oz herb butter
- 1 lemon, cut into wedges

Method

1. Season the lamb chops with a little salt and pepper
2. Add the butter to the pan and wait to melt
3. Fry the lamb chops in each side for around 4 minutes, depending on thickness
4. Arrange on a serving plate with a chunk of herb butter and a lemon wedge

Calories 729, Fat 62g, Carbs 0.3g, Protein 43g

134. Beef & Eggplant Casserole

Time: 15 minutes | Serves 2

Ingredients:

- 1 eggplant peeled, cut lengthwise
- ½ cup lean ground beef
- 1 onion, chopped
- 1 tsp olive oil
- ¼ tsp. freshly ground black pepper
- 1 tomato
- 2 tbsp. freshly chopped parsley

Method

1. Place eggplants in a bowl and Season with salt. Let sit for 10 minutes. Rinse well and drain.
2. Grease the inner pot with oil. Stir-fry onions for 2 minutes, until soft. Add ground beef, tomato, and cook for 5 minutes.
3. Remove from the pot and Transfer to a deep bowl.
4. Make a layer with eggplant slices in the pot. Spread the ground beef mixture over and sprinkle with parsley.
5. Make another layer with eggplants and repeat until you've used up all Ingredients.
6. Seal the lid and cook on High Pressure for 12 minutes. Do a quick release.

Per Serving:

Calories 331, Fat 25g, Carbs 11g, Fiber 4g, Protein 16g

135.   Crusted Herb Pork Chops

Time: 13 minutes | Serves 2

Ingredients:

- 1 tablespoon olive Oil
- ½ teaspoon pepper
- ½ teaspoon salt
- 1 tablespoon parsley
- 1 tablespoon thyme
- ½ cup panko breadcrumbs
- 1 tablespoon dijon mustard
- 2 pork chops

Method

1. Begin by heating your oven to 450°F. Next, you will prep your pork chops by rubbing them with the Dijon mustard.
2. In a small bowl, combine the salt, pepper, parsley, thyme, and panko breadcrumbs. For a healthier version, try to get whole wheat breadcrumbs.
3. When you are ready, dip the mustard covered pork chops into the breadcrumbs. Be sure that they are coated evenly.
4. Once they are ready, go ahead and heat a large skillet over medium heat and put your olive oil in.
5. Sauté the chops for two or three minutes on each side before popping it into the oven.
6. Keep the pork chops in the oven for eight to ten minutes before removing and allowing to cool.
7. Portion into your containers and serve with your favorite side.

Per Serving:

Calories 445, Fat 25g, Carbs 31g, Protein 25g

136. Spicy Lamb Burgers with Harissa Mayo

Time: 10 minutes | Serves 2

Ingredients:

- ½ small onion, minced
- 1 garlic clove, minced
- 2 teaspoons minced fresh parsley
- 2 teaspoons minced fresh mint
- ¼ teaspoon salt
- Pinch freshly ground black pepper
- 1 teaspoon cumin
- 1 teaspoon smoked paprika
- ¼ teaspoon coriander
- 8 ounces' lean ground lamb
- 2 tablespoons olive oil mayonnaise
- ½ teaspoon harissa paste (more or less to taste)
- 2 hamburger buns or pitas
- fresh greens,
- tomato slices (optional, for serving)

Method

1. Preheat the grill to medium-high (350–400°F) and oil the grill grate. Alternatively, you can cook these in a heavy pan (cast iron is best) on the stovetop.
2. In a large bowl, combine the onion, garlic, parsley, mint, salt, pepper, cumin, paprika, and coriander. Add the lamb and, using your hands, combine the meat with the spices so they are evenly distributed. Form meat mixture into 2 patties.
3. Grill the burgers for 4 minutes per side, or until the internal temperature registers 160°F for medium.
4. If cooking on the stovetop, heat the pan to medium-high and oil the pan. Cook the burgers for 5 to 6 minutes per side, or until the internal temperature registers 160°F.
5. While the burgers are cooking, combine the mayonnaise and harissa in a small bowl.

6. Serve the burgers with the harissa mayonnaise and slices of tomato and fresh greens on a bun or pita—or skip the bun altogether.

Per Serving:

Calories: 381; Fat: 20g; Carbs: 27g; Protein: 22g

137.   Greek-Style Ground Beef Pita Sandwiches

Time: 10 minutes | Serves 2

Ingredients:

For the beef

- 1 tablespoon olive oil
- ½ medium onion, minced
- 2 garlic cloves, minced
- 6 ounces' lean ground beef
- 1 teaspoon dried oregano

For the yogurt sauce

- ⅓ cup plain Greek yogurt
- 1 ounce crumbled feta cheese (about 3 tablespoons)
- 1 tablespoon minced fresh parsley
- 1 tablespoon minced scallion
- 1 tablespoon freshly squeezed lemon juice
- Pinch salt

For the sandwiches

- 2 large Greek-style pitas
- ½ cup cherry tomatoes, halved
- 1 cup diced cucumber
- Salt
- Freshly ground black pepper

Method

1. Heat the olive oil in a sauté pan over medium high-heat. Add the onion, garlic, and ground beef and sauté for 7 minutes, breaking up the meat well.
2. When the meat is no longer pink, drain off any fat and stir in the oregano. Turn off the heat. To make the yogurt sauce
3. In a small bowl, combine the yogurt, feta, parsley, scallion, lemon juice, and salt. To assemble the sandwiches
4. Warm the pitas in the microwave for 20 seconds each.
5. To serve, spread some of the yogurt sauce over each warm pita. Top with the ground beef, cherry tomatoes, and diced cucumber. Season with salt and pepper. Add additional yogurt sauce if desired.

Per Serving:

Calories: 541; fat: 21g; carbs: 57g; Protein: 29g

138.   Pork Souvlaki Pita

Time: 15 minutes | Serves 2

Ingredients:

- 1 pound (boneless, skinless) pork loin, diced into 1-inch cubes
- 2 tablespoons olive oil Juice of
- 1 lemon
- 1 garlic clove, minced
- 1 teaspoon dried oregano
- Salt and pepper, to taste
- Tomato slices and sliced red onion

for serving

- 4 pita bread

For the tzatziki

- 1 cucumber, peeled and finely diced

- 1 garlic clove, minced
- 2 tablespoons olive oil
- 2 cups Greek yogurt
- Kosher salt, to taste
- 1 tablespoon red wine vinegar

Method

1. In a large mixing bowl, combine the cubed pork, salt, pepper, olive oil, lemon juice, garlic, salt, and pepper.
2. Insert the marinated pork cubes on metal or wooden skewers.
3. Heat a large, nonstick grill pan over medium heat. Cook the pork on each side for 5-7 minutes.
4. combine the Greek yogurt, cucumber, garlic, olive oil, red wine vinegar, and salt in a medium mixing bowl.
5. Spread each pita generously with tzatziki sauce, top evenly with pork cubes, garnish with tomato and onion.
6. Fold the pita to make a roll, wrap in parchment paper or foil, if desired, and serve warm.

Per Serving:

Calories 559, Fat 24g, Carbs 14g, Protein 69g

139.   Spiced Lamb and Beef Kebabs

Time: 10 minutes | Serves 2

Ingredients:

- ½ pound ground beef
- 1 teaspoon ground cumin
- 1 small onion, finely grated
- ½ pound ground lamb
- ½ teaspoon ground coriander
- 1 teaspoon smoked paprika
- 2 garlic cloves, minced

- 2 tablespoons fresh parsley, finely chopped
- ¼ cayenne pepper (adjust based on spice preference)
- Salt and black pepper, to taste
- 1 tablespoon olive oil, for grilling

Method

1. In a large mixing bowl, combine the ground lamb, ground beef, grated onion, minced garlic, chopped parsley, cumin, smoked paprika, coriander, cayenne pepper, salt, and black pepper. Mix thoroughly until all ingredients are well blended.
2. Cover and refrigerate the meat mixture for at least 1 hour, or up to 4 hours, to allow the flavors to meld.
3. Preheat a grill or grill pan to medium-high heat.
4. Divide the meat mixture into equal portions and shape each portion around skewers to form kebabs. If using wooden skewers, make sure to soak them in water for at least 30 minutes prior to grilling to prevent burning.
5. Brush the grill with olive oil to prevent sticking. Place the kebabs on the hot grill.
6. Grill the kebabs, turning occasionally, until evenly browned and cooked through, about 10 minutes. Serve the kebabs hot, straight off the grill.

Per Serving

Calories: 517; Fat: 25g; Carbs: 5g; Protein: 38g

140.   Sage Pork Chops with Sweet & Spicy Chutney

Time: 15 minutes | Serves 2

Ingredients:

- 2 tablespoons olive oil
- 4 sage leaves, finely chopped
- 2 pork chops, about 1 inch thick
- Salt and black pepper, to taste

For the Sweet & Spicy Chutney:

- ½ cup fresh mango, diced
- ¼ cup red bell pepper, diced
- 1 small red onion, finely chopped
- 2 tablespoons apple cider vinegar
- 1 tablespoon brown sugar
- ½ teaspoon red pepper flakes (adjust to taste)
- Season the pork chops with salt, pepper, and chopped sage.

Method

1. Heat the olive oil in a skillet over medium-high heat. Add the pork chops and cook for about 6-7 minutes on each side, or until they are golden brown and cooked to an internal temperature of 145°F.
2. While the pork chops are cooking, make the chutney. Combine the mango, red bell pepper, red onion, apple cider vinegar, brown sugar, red pepper flakes, and a pinch of salt in a small saucepan.
3. Cook over medium heat, stirring occasionally, until the mixture has thickened and the ingredients are soft, about 10-15 minutes.
4. Remove the pork chops from the skillet and let them rest for a few minutes. Serve the pork chops with a generous spoonful of the sweet and spicy chutney on top.

Per Serving:

Calories: 400, Fat: 21g, Carbs: 18g, Protein: 39g

Fish & Seafood

141. Pesto Fish Fillet

Time: 15 minutes | Serves 2

Ingredients:

- 2 fish fillets about 6 ounces each
- 2 tablespoons pesto
- 1 tablespoon olive oil
- Salt and black pepper, to taste

Optional:

- lemon wedges for serving

Method

1. Preheat your oven to 400°F (200°C). Season the fish fillets with salt and freshly ground black pepper.
2. Spread 1 tablespoon of pesto on each fillet, coating evenly.
3. Heat the olive oil in an oven-safe skillet over medium heat. Once hot, add the fish fillets, skin-side down if they have skin.
4. Cook for 2-3 minutes until the bottom starts to turn golden.
5. Transfer the skillet to the preheated oven and bake for about 10-12 minutes, or until the fish is cooked through and flakes easily with a fork.
6. Serve immediately, with lemon wedges on the side if desired.

Per Serving:

Calories: 326; Fat: 16 g; Carbs: 1 g; Protein: 31.8 g

142. Salmon and Mango Mix

Time: 15 minutes | Serves 2

Ingredients:

- 2 salmon fillets, about 6 ounces each
- Salt and pepper to the taste
- 1 tablespoon olive oil
- ½ small onion, finely chopped
- 1 ripe mango, peeled and diced
- 1 red bell pepper, diced
- 1 tablespoon chopped fresh cilantro
- Juice of 1 lime

Method

1. Season the salmon fillets with salt and freshly ground black pepper.
2. Heat the olive oil in a skillet over medium-high heat. Add the salmon fillets, skin-side down, and cook for about 6-7 minutes, or until the skin is crispy.
3. Flip the fillets and cook on the other side for another 6-7 minutes, or until the salmon is cooked through and flakes easily with a fork.
4. While the salmon is cooking, combine the diced mango, red bell pepper, red onion, lime juice, and cilantro in a bowl. Mix well to combine. Season with salt.
5. Serve the cooked salmon with a generous topping of the mango mix.
6. Garnish with additional cilantro if desired.

Per Serving:

Calories: 351; Fat: 18.9g; Carbs: 22.4g; Protein: 32.4g

143.   Trout and Tzatziki Sauce

Time: 10 minutes | Serves 2

Ingredients:

- Salt and black pepper, to taste
- 2 trout fillets, about 6 ounces each
- 1 tablespoon olive oil
- ½ cucumber, grated and excess water squeezed out
- 1 small garlic clove, minced
- 1 tablespoon chopped fresh dill

- Juice of ½ lemon
- 1 cup Greek yogurt

Method

1. Season the trout fillets with salt and black pepper.
2. Heat the olive oil in a skillet over medium-high heat. Once hot, add the trout fillets, skin-side down, and cook for about 4-5 minutes until the skin is crispy.
3. Flip the fillets and cook for another 3-4 minutes, or until the trout is cooked through and flakes easily with a fork.
4. While the trout is cooking, prepare the tzatziki sauce. In a bowl, combine the grated cucumber, Greek yogurt, minced garlic, chopped dill, and lemon juice. Mix well until smooth. Season with salt and black pepper to taste.
5. Serve the cooked trout with a generous dollop of tzatziki sauce on the side.
6. Garnish with additional dill or lemon slices if desired.

Per Serving:

Calories: 343; Fat: 18.5g; Carbs: 8.3g; Protein: 39.6g

144.   Lemon-Parsley Swordfish

Time: 10 minutes | Serves 2

Ingredients:

- 2 tablespoons fresh parsley, finely chopped
- Juice of 1 lemon
- 2 tablespoons olive oil
- 1 garlic clove, minced
- Salt and freshly ground black pepper, to taste
- 2 swordfish steaks (about 6 ounces)

Optional:

- Additional lemon slices for serving

Method

1. Season the swordfish steaks generously with salt and pepper on both sides. Heat the olive oil in a skillet over medium-high heat.
2. Once the oil is hot, add the swordfish steaks to the skillet. Cook for about 4-5 minutes on each side, or until the fish is cooked through and easily flakes with a fork.
3. While the fish is cooking, in a small bowl, mix together the lemon juice, chopped parsley, and minced garlic.
4. Once the swordfish is cooked, remove the steaks from the skillet and place them on a serving platter.
5. Pour the lemon-parsley mixture over the cooked swordfish steaks while they are still hot. Serve immediately, garnished with additional lemon slices if desired.

Per Serving

Calories: 326; Fat: 20.7g; Protein: 34.2g; Carbs: 2.9g

145.   Grilled Octopus

Time: 10 minutes | Serves 2

Ingredients:

- Fresh parsley chopped, for garnish
- 1-pound octopus, cleaned and pre-cooked
- Juice of 1 lemon
- Salt and fresh ground black pepper, to taste
- 1 teaspoon dried oregano
- 2 garlic cloves, minced
- 2 tablespoons olive oil
- Lemon wedges, for serving

Method

1. If the octopus is not pre-cooked, boil it in lightly salted water for about 45-60 minutes or until tender. Allow it to cool, then proceed with the following steps. Cut the pre-cooked octopus into pieces suitable for grilling.

2. In a bowl, combine olive oil, minced garlic, dried oregano, lemon juice, salt, and black pepper to create a marinade.
3. Toss the octopus pieces in the marinade and let sit for at least 30 minutes to absorb the flavors.
4. a grill or grill pan over medium-high heat. Remove the octopus from the marinade, letting excess drip off (reserve the marinade for basting).
5. Grill the octopus pieces for about 3-5 minutes on each side, basting occasionally with the marinade, until they are charred and heated through.
6. Serve the grilled octopus garnished with chopped parsley and accompanied by lemon wedges.

Per Serving

Calories: 296; Fat: 9g; Carbs: 8.1g; Protein: 34.2g

146.   Spaghetti with Tuna and Capers

Time: 15 minutes | Serves 2

Ingredients:

- 1 garlic clove, minced
- Fresh parsley, chopped for garnish
- 2 tablespoons capers, rinsed
- 1 can (6 ounces) tuna in olive oil, drained
- 6ounces spaghetti
- Salt and freshly ground black pepper, to taste
- 2 tablespoons olive oil
- Juice of 1 lemon

Method

1. Bring a large pot of salted water to a boil. Add the spaghetti and cook according to the package instructions until al dente. Drain and set aside, reserving 1/2 cup of the pasta cooking water.
2. While the pasta is cooking, heat the olive oil in a large skillet over medium heat. Add the minced garlic and sauté until fragrant, about 1 minute.

3. Add the drained tuna and capers to the skillet. Cook for 2-3 minutes, breaking up the tuna into flakes.
4. Stir in the lemon juice and reserved pasta water. Season with salt and black pepper.
5. Add the drained spaghetti to the skillet. Toss well to coat the pasta with the sauce and heat everything through. Serve the spaghetti garnished with chopped parsley.

Per Serving

Calories: 390; Fat: 14g; Carbs: 46.8g; Protein: 23.6g

147.   Crusty Halibut

Time: 15 minutes | Serves 2

Ingredients:

- ½ cup panko breadcrumbs
- 1 egg, beaten
- 2 tablespoons olive oil
- Salt and pepper, to taste
- 2 halibut fillets, about 6 ounces for each
- Lemon wedges, for serving
- ¼ cup all-purpose flour

Method

1. Season the halibut fillets with salt and black pepper. Place the flour, beaten egg, and panko breadcrumbs in three separate shallow dishes.
2. Dredge each fillet in the flour, shaking off excess, then dip in the beaten egg, and finally coat thoroughly with panko breadcrumbs.
3. Heat the olive oil in a skillet over medium-high heat. Once hot, add the breaded halibut fillets.
4. Cook the fillets for about 6-7 minutes on each side, or until the crust is golden and crispy and the fish is cooked through.

5. Transfer the cooked halibut to plates and squeeze fresh lemon juice over the top before serving.

Per Serving:

Calories: 373, Fat: 17.2g, Carbs: 15g, Protein: 39g

148.   Smokey Glazed Tuna

Time: 15 minutes | Serves 2

Ingredients:

- 2 tuna steaks (about 6 ounce each)
- 1 tablespoon olive oil
- Salt and black pepper, to taste
- *For the glaze:*
- 2 tablespoons honey
- 1 garlic clove, minced
- 1 tablespoon soy sauce
- 1 teaspoon smoked paprika

Optional:

- ½ teaspoon chili powder

Method

1. In a small bowl, whisk together the honey, soy sauce, smoked paprika, minced garlic, and optional chili powder to make the glaze.
2. Season the tuna steaks with salt and pepper. Heat the olive oil in a grill pan or skillet over medium-high heat.
3. Brush the tuna steaks with half of the glaze and place them in the hot pan.
4. Grill the tuna for about 3 minutes on each side for medium-rare, or adjust the cooking time based on your preferred doneness.
5. Halfway through cooking, brush the remaining glaze over the tuna steaks.
6. Once cooked to your liking, remove the tuna steaks from the pan and let them rest for a few minutes.

7. Serve the tuna steaks immediately, garnished with extra sauce from the pan if desired.

Per Serving:

Calories: 300; Fat: 7.9g; Carbs: 17g; Protein: 47.4g

149.   Mussels O' Marine

Time: 10 minutes | Serves 2

Ingredients:

- 2 pounds of fresh Mussels, clean and debearded
- 2 tablespoons olive oil
- 1 small onion, finely chopped
- 2 garlic cloves, minced
- ½ cup vegetable broth
- ½ cup white wine
- 1 tablespoon fresh parsley, chopped
- 1 tablespoon fresh thyme leaves
- Salt and black pepper, to taste

Optional:

- fresh lemon wedges for serving
- ½ teaspoon red pepper flakes for a spicy kick

Method

1. In a large pot, heat the olive oil over medium heat. Add the minced garlic and chopped onion, sautéing until the onion is translucent and the garlic is fragrant, about 2-3 minutes.
2. Increase the heat to high, and add the white wine and vegetable broth. Bring the mixture to a boil.
3. Add the cleaned mussels to the boiling broth. Cover the pot and let the mussels steam until they open, about 5-7 minutes. Discard any mussels that do not open.

4. Once cooked, sprinkle the mussels with chopped parsley, thyme, and optional red pepper flakes. Season with salt and black pepper to taste.
5. Gently stir the mussels to distribute the herbs and seasoning evenly.
6. Serve the mussels hot, with the broth from the pot and optional lemon wedges on the side.

Per Serving:

Calories: 283; Fat: 14g; Carbs: 16g; Protein: 29g

150.   Hot and Fresh Fishy Steaks

Time: 15 minutes | Serves 2

Ingredients:

- 2 fish steaks (such as salmon, tuna), about 6 ounces
- 1 garlic clove, minced
- Juice of 1 lemon
- 1 teaspoon paprika
- 1 teaspoon chili powder
- Salt and black pepper, to taste
- 2 tablespoons olive oil

Optional:

- Fresh herbs such as parsley or cilantro, chopped for garnish
- A pinch of cayenne pepper for extra heat

Method

1. Season the fish steaks with salt, black pepper, chili powder, and paprika. Rub the minced garlic evenly over each steak.
2. Heat the olive oil in a skillet over medium-high heat. Once the oil is hot, place the fish steaks in the skillet.

3. Cook the steaks for about 4-5 minutes on each side, depending on thickness, or until they are cooked through and easily flake with a fork.
4. Just before removing from the heat, squeeze lemon juice over the cooked fish steaks to enhance the flavors.
5. If using, sprinkle a pinch of cayenne pepper over the steaks for added spiciness.
6. Garnish with chopped fresh herbs if desired. Serve immediately

Per Serving:

Calories: 412, Fat: 19.4g, Carbs: 35.6g, Protein: 25.7g

151. Garlic & Lemon Sea Bass

Time: 12 minutes | Serves 2

Ingredients:

- 2 tablespoons olive oil
- 2 sea bass fillets (about 6 ounces each)
- Juice of 1 lemon
- 2 garlic cloves, finely minced
- Salt and black pepper, to taste
- Zest of ½ lemon
- 1 tablespoon fresh parsley, chopped

Method

1. Season the sea bass fillets with salt and pepper. Heat the olive oil in a skillet over medium heat.
2. Once hot, add the minced garlic and sauté for about 1 minute until fragrant but not browned.
3. Add the sea bass fillets to the skillet, skin side down if they have skin. Cook for about 5-6 minutes on one side until the skin is crisp and golden.
4. Flip the fillets carefully and cook for another 5-6 minutes, or until the fish is opaque and flakes easily with a fork.

5. Remove the skillet from heat. Drizzle the lemon juice over the fillets and sprinkle with lemon zest.
6. Garnish with chopped fresh parsley before serving.

Per Serving:

Calories: 230, Fat: 20g, Carbs: 3g, Protein: 34g

152.   Crispy Garlic Shrimp

Time: 10 minutes | Serves 2

Ingredients:

1. ½ lb. raw shrimp, peeled and deveined
2. 1 garlic clove, minced
3. ¼ tsp. anise seeds
4. 1 Tbsp. unsalted butter
5. Salt and black pepper, to taste
6. 1 Tbsp. fresh parsley, finely chopped
7. 2 lemon wedges, for sprinkling

Method

1. Combine shrimp with garlic, anise seeds, salt, and pepper.
2. Melt butter in a frying pan.
3. Add shrimp and cook for 10 minutes until golden, stirring occasionally.
4. Sprinkle with chopped parsley and lemon juice.
5. Serve crispy garlic shrimp in a sauce with pasta, rice, and beans as an ingredient in a salad or cocktail, an appetizer, or a separate dish.

Per Serving:

Calories: 172, Fat: 5.1g, Carbs: 3.9g, Protein: 27g

153. Salmon with Vegetables

Time: 10 minutes | Serves 2

Ingredients:

- 2 salmon/white fish fillets (6 oz. each)
- Olive oil and unsalted butter
- 1 Tbsp. lemon juice, for sprinkling

For the Marinade

- 1 Tbsp. olive oil
- 2 Tbsp. lemon juice
- 1 garlic clove, crushed
- 1 Tbsp. dried oregano/fresh chopped oregano

For the Salad

- 2 tomatoes, chopped
- 1 small bell pepper, chopped
- 1 small red onion, diced
- 1 cup lettuce, chopped
- ½ cup feta cheese, cubed
- 1 Tbsp. olive oil
- ½ Tbsp. white wine vinegar
- ½ Tbsp. fresh lemon juice
- ½ tsp. dried rosemary
- Salt, to taste

Method

1. Mix all the ingredients for the marinade in a bowl and coat the salmon fillets in it. Let the salmon marinate for 20 minutes.
2. Heat olive oil and butter in a frying pan over medium-high heat. Fry marinated salmon fillets for 8 minutes until golden brown, flipping once.
3. Combine all the vegetables for the salad and add feta cheese on top. You can replace the fresh vegetables with roasted or baked ones for a smoky flavor.
4. Mix all the ingredients for the dressing in a small bowl. Pour it over the salad.

5. Transfer the salad on a serving platter and serve with the salmon.

Per Serving:

Calories: 449, Fat: 29 g, Carbs: 12.3 g, Protein: 41 g

154.   Baked White Fish with Vegetables

Time: 15 minutes | Serves 2

Ingredients:

- 1 lb. white fish filet (halibut/cod)
- Salt and pepper, to taste
- 2 Tbsp. olive oil
- 1 lemon, juiced
- 6 cherry tomatoes
- ½ medium zucchini, chopped
- 1 small carrot, chopped
- 2 tbsp. red onion, diced
- 3 garlic cloves, minced
- 1 Tbsp. fresh parsley
- 2 tsp. dried basil

Method

1. Preheat the oven to 425°F (218°C). Grease a baking dish with olive oil.
2. Pat white fish dry and season with salt and pepper. Arrange the fish on the baking dish and sprinkle with lemon juice.
3. Coat the fish with vegetables and season with salt and pepper.
4. Bake for 15–20 minutes, stirring halfway through.
5. Serve sprinkled with fresh lemon juice and chopped parsley.

Per Serving:

Calories: 460, Fat: 20 g, Carbs: 23 g, Protein: 49 g

155.   Garlic Scallops

Time: 12 minutes | Serves 2

Ingredients:

- ½ lb. dry sea scallops
- 1 garlic clove, minced
- ½ Tbsp. lemon juice
- 1 Tbsp. fresh rosemary, chopped
- 1 Tbsp. ghee/butter, melted
- ¼ tsp. smoked paprika
- 1 Tbsp. olive oil
- Salt and pepper, to taste
- lemon slices and watercress, for garnish

Method

1. Season scallops with salt and pepper. Melt butter in a skillet over medium heat. Add minced garlic.
2. Place scallops in a single layer in the skillet. Fry for 5 minutes until golden, flipping once. Take care not to overcook them.
3. Combine lemon juice, paprika, chopped basil, olive oil, salt, and pepper in a bowl.
4. Transfer scallops to a serving platter and sprinkle with the lemon dressing. Garnish with watercress and lemon slices.
5. Serve with roasted asparagus, Brussels sprouts, cauliflower, or your favorite dipping sauce.

Per Serving:

Calories: 119, Fat: 2.5 g, Carbs: 5.4 g, Protein: 22 g

156.   Dill Chutney Salmon

Time: 8 minutes | Serves 2

Ingredients:

Chutney:

- ¼ cup fresh dill
- ¼ cup extra virgin olive oil
- Juice from ½ lemon
- Sea salt, to taste

Fish:

- 2 cups water
- 2 salmon fillets
- Juice from ½ lemon
- ¼ teaspoon paprika
- Salt and freshly ground pepper to taste

Method

1. Pulse all the chutney ingredients in a food processor until creamy. Set aside.
2. Add the water and steamer basket to the Instant Pot. Place salmon fillets, skin-side down, on the steamer basket.
3. Drizzle the lemon juice over salmon and sprinkle with the paprika. Secure the lid.
4. Select the Manual mode and set the cooking time for 3 minutes at High Pressure.
5. Once cooking is complete, do a quick pressure release. Carefully open the lid.
6. Season the fillets with pepper and salt to taste. Serve topped with the dill chutney.

Per Serving

Calories: 636, Fat: 41.1g, Carbs: 1.9g, Protein: 65.3g

157.   Garlic-Butter Parmesan Salmon and Asparagus

Time: 15 minutes | Serves 2

Ingredients:

- 2 (6-ounce) salmon fillets, skin on and patted dry
- Pink Himalayan salt
- Freshly ground black pepper, to taste
- 1-pound fresh asparagus, ends snapped off
- 3 tablespoons almond butter
- 2 garlic cloves, minced
- ¼ cup grated Parmesan cheese

Method

1. Preheat the oven to 400°F. Line a baking sheet with aluminum foil. Season both sides of the salmon fillets with salt and pepper.
2. Put the salmon in the middle of the baking sheet and arrange the asparagus around the salmon.
3. Heat the almond butter in a small saucepan over medium heat. Add the minced garlic and cook for about 3 minutes, or until the garlic just begins to brown.
4. Drizzle the garlic-butter sauce over the salmon and asparagus and scatter the Parmesan cheese on top.
5. Bake in the preheated oven for about 12 minutes, or until the salmon is cooked through and the asparagus is crisp-tender.
6. You can switch the oven to broil at the end of cooking time for about 3 minutes to get a nice char on the asparagus. Let cool for 5 minutes before serving.

Per Serving

Calories: 435, Fat: 26.1g, Carbs: 10.0g, Protein: 42.3g

158.   Grilled Lemon Pesto Salmon

Time: 15 minutes | Serves 2

Ingredients:

- 10 ounces' salmon fillet (1 large piece or 2 smaller ones)
- Salt and freshly ground black pepper, to taste
- 2 tablespoons prepared pesto sauce
- 1 large fresh lemon, sliced
- Cooking spray

Method

- Preheat the grill to medium-high heat. Spray the grill grates with cooking spray.
- Season the salmon with salt and black pepper. Spread the pesto sauce on top.
- Make a bed of fresh lemon slices about the same size as the salmon fillet on the hot grill, and place the salmon on top of the lemon slices.
- Put any additional lemon slices on top of the salmon.
- Grill the salmon for 6 to 10 minutes, or until the fish is opaque and flakes apart easily. Serve hot.

Per Serving

Calories: 316, Fat: 21.1g, Carbs: 1.0g, Protein: 29.0g

159. Steamed Trout with Lemon Herb Crust

Time: 15 minutes | Serves 2

Ingredients:

- 3 tablespoons olive oil

- 3 garlic cloves, chopped
- 2 tablespoons fresh lemon juice
- 1 tablespoon chopped fresh mint
- 1 tablespoon chopped fresh parsley
- ¼ teaspoon dried ground thyme
- 1 teaspoon sea salt
- 1-pound fresh trout (2 pieces)
- 2 cups fish stock

Method

1. Stir together the olive oil, garlic, lemon juice, mint, parsley, thyme, and salt in a small bowl. Brush the marinade onto the fish.
2. Insert a trivet in the Instant Pot. Pour in the fish stock and place the fish on the trivet.
3. Secure the lid. Select the Steam mode and set the cooking time for 15 minutes at High Pressure.
4. Once cooking is complete, do a quick pressure release. Carefully open the lid. Serve warm.

Per Serving

calories: 477, fat: 29.6g, carbs: 3.6g, protein: 51.7g

160.   Tomato Tuna Melts

Time: 15 minutes | Serves 2

Ingredients:

- 1 (5-ounce) can chunk light tuna packed in water, drained
- 2 tablespoons plain Greek yogurt
- 2 tablespoons finely chopped celery
- 1 tablespoon finely chopped red onion
- 2 teaspoons freshly squeezed
- lemon juice Pinch cayenne pepper
- 1 large tomato, cut into ¾-inch-thick rounds
- ½ cup shredded Cheddar Cheese

Method

1. Preheat the broiler to High. Stir together the tuna, yogurt, celery, red onion, lemon juice, and cayenne pepper in a medium bowl.
2. Place the tomato rounds on a baking sheet.
3. Top each with some tuna salad and Cheddar cheese.

4. Broil for 3 to 4 minutes until the cheese is melted and bubbly. Cool for 5 minutes before serving.

Per Serving

calories: 244, fat: 10.0g, carbs: 6.9g, protein: 30.1g

Snacks

161.   Mediterranean Chickpea Salad

Time: 15 minutes | Serves 2

Ingredients:

For the Salad:

- 1 can (15 ounces) chickpeas, drained and rinsed
- 1 cup cherry tomatoes, halved
- 1/2 cucumber, diced
- 1/4 red onion, finely chopped
- 1/4 cup chopped fresh parsley
- 1/4 cup chopped fresh mint leaves (optional)
- 1/4 cup crumbled feta cheese (optional)
- Kalamata olives, pitted and halved (optional)

For the Dressing:

- 3 tablespoons extra-virgin olive oil
- 1 tablespoon freshly squeezed lemon juice
- 1 clove garlic, minced
- ½ teaspoon dried oregano
- Salt and pepper to taste

Method

1. Drain and rinse the canned chickpeas thoroughly under cold running water. This helps remove excess salt and improves the texture.
2. In a large salad bowl, combine the chickpeas, halved cherry tomatoes, diced cucumber, finely chopped red onion, chopped fresh parsley, and optional chopped fresh mint leaves.
3. In a small bowl, whisk together the extra-virgin olive oil, freshly squeezed lemon juice, minced garlic, dried oregano, salt, and pepper to taste. Adjust the

seasoning according to your preference.

4. Pour the dressing over the salad ingredients in the large salad bowl. Toss everything together until well combined and evenly coated with the dressing.
5. If desired, you can add crumbled feta cheese and halved Kalamata olives to the salad for extra Mediterranean flavor.
6. Refrigerate the chickpea salad for about 30 minutes before serving to allow the flavors to meld together. It can be served cold or at room temperature.

Per Serving

Calories: 385 Kcal, Fat: 19g, Carbs: 43g, Protein: 11g

162.   Authentic Mediterranean Hummus

Time: 15 minutes | Serves 2

Ingredients:

- 1 can (15 ounces) chickpeas (garbanzo beans), drained and rinsed
- 1/4 cup fresh lemon juice (about 1 large lemon)
- 1/4 cup tahini (sesame paste)
- 1 small garlic clove, minced
- 2 tablespoons extra-virgin olive oil, plus more for drizzling
- 1/2 teaspoon ground cumin
- Salt, to taste
- 2 tablespoons water (or more, for desired consistency)

Optional toppings:

- Paprika,
- Chopped fresh parsley
- Pine nuts

Method

1. Drain and rinse the canned chickpeas thoroughly under cold running water. This helps remove excess salt and improves the texture.
2. In a food processor, combine the drained chickpeas, fresh lemon juice, tahini, minced garlic, ground cumin, and a pinch of salt.

3. Process the mixture until it becomes a coarse paste, stopping to scrape down the sides of the bowl as needed.
4. With the food processor running, add 2 tablespoons of water and 2 tablespoons of extra-virgin olive oil. Continue to process until the hummus becomes smooth and creamy. You can add more water if you prefer a thinner consistency.
5. the hummus and adjust the seasoning by adding more salt or lemon juice if needed. Blend again to incorporate any additional ingredients.
6. Transfer the hummus to a serving bowl. Create a well in the center and drizzle with extra olive oil. If desired, garnish with a sprinkle of paprika, chopped fresh parsley, or pine nuts.
7. Serve the authentic Mediterranean hummus with pita bread, fresh vegetables, or your favorite dipping options.

Per Serving

Calories: 260 Kcal, Fat: 18g, Carbs: 20g, Protein: 8g

163.   Hummus with Parsley and Pita

Time: 10 minutes | Serves 2

Ingredients:

- 1 cup canned chickpeas, rinsed and drained
- 2 tablespoons tahini
- 1 clove garlic, minced
- 2 tablespoons fresh lemon juice
- 2 tablespoons olive oil
- 1/4 cup fresh parsley, chopped
- Salt and pepper to taste
- 2 whole wheat pita breads for serving

Method

1. Combine chickpeas, tahini, garlic, lemon juice, and olive oil in a food processor. Blend until smooth.

2. Season with salt and pepper to taste.
3. Transfer to a serving dish.
4. Garnish with chopped parsley. Drizzle with additional olive oil if desired.
5. Warm the pita bread slightly in a toaster or oven. Serve alongside the hummus.

Per Serving

Calories: 356, Fat: 16g, Carbs: 45g, Protein: 12g

164.   Feta Cheese Cubes with Herbs and Olives

Time: 10 minutes | Serves 2

Ingredients:

- 0.4lb. feta cheese, cut into cubes
- ¼ cup mixed fresh herbs (e.g., dill, parsley, oregano)
- ½ cup olives (mix of green and black)
- 2 tablespoons olive oil
- 1 teaspoon lemon zest
- ½ teaspoon cracked black pepper

Method

1. In a mixing bowl, gently toss the feta cheese cubes with the olive oil, lemon zest, and cracked black pepper.
2. Carefully fold in the mixed herbs until the feta cubes are evenly coated.
3. Arrange the herbed feta cubes on a serving plate and scatter the olives around them.
4. Serve immediately or cover and refrigerate for 1 hour to enhance the flavors.

Per Serving

Calories: 250, Fat: 21g, Carbs: 6g, Protein: 9g

165.   Fried Spicy Shrimps

Time: 10 minutes | Serves 2

Ingredients:

- 04 Ib. large shrimps, peeled and deveined
- 2 cloves garlic, minced
- 1 tsp red chili flakes
- 2 tbsp. olive oil
- 1 tbsp. fresh lemon juice
- 1 tsp dried oregano
- Salt and pepper, to taste
- Fresh parsley, chopped (for garnish)

Method

1. Mix shrimp with garlic, chili flakes, lemon juice, oregano, salt, and pepper in a bowl.
2. Heat olive oil in a pan over medium-high heat.
3. Add shrimp mixture and cook for 4-5 minutes on each side, until shrimp turn pink and are slightly crispy.
4. Garnish with fresh parsley before serving.

Per Serving

Calories: 220, Fat: 12g, Carbs: 3g, Protein: 24g

166.   Grilled Sardines on Toast

Time: 10 minutes | Serves 2

Ingredients:

- 4 fresh sardines, cleaned and gutted
- 2 slices of whole-grain bread
- 1 garlic clove, halved
- 2 tablespoons of olive oil

- Juice of 1 lemon
- Salt and pepper to taste
- Fresh parsley for garnish

Method

1. Preheat the grill to medium-high heat. Season the sardines with salt, pepper, and lemon juice.
2. Grill the sardines on each side for 3-4 minutes or until cooked. Toast the bread slices until golden brown.
3. Rub the toasted bread with the halved garlic clove. Drizzle olive oil over the toasted bread.
4. Place the grilled sardines on the toasted bread. Garnish with fresh parsley and serve immediately.

Per Serving

Calories: 310, Fat: 14g, Carbs: 23g, Protein: 25g

167. Squash and Zucchini Fritters

Time: 10 minutes | Serves 2

Ingredients:

- 1 small zucchini, grated
- 1 small yellow squash, grated
- 2 tablespoons all-purpose flour
- 1 egg, beaten
- 2 tablespoons feta cheese, crumbled
- 1 tablespoon fresh dill, chopped
- Salt and pepper to taste
- Olive oil for frying

Method

1. In a bowl, combine grated zucchini and squash with a pinch of salt. Let sit for 10 minutes, then squeeze out excess moisture.

2. Add flour, beaten egg, feta cheese, dill, salt, and pepper to the squash mixture. Stir until well combined.
3. Heat olive oil in a skillet over medium heat. Spoon the fritter mixture into the skillet, flattening slightly.
4. Cook until golden brown, about 5 minutes per side.
5. Transfer cakes to a paper towel-lined plate to drain excess oil.

Per Serving

Calories: 150, Fat: 8g, Carbs: 15g, Protein: 6g

168.   Mediterranean Trail Mix

Time: 10 minutes | Serves 2

Ingredients:

- 1 tablespoon olive oil
- 1 tablespoon maple syrup
- 1 teaspoon vanilla
- ½ teaspoon cardamom
- ½ teaspoon allspice
- 2 cups mixed, unsalted nuts
- ¼ cup unsalted pumpkin or sunflower seeds
- ½ cup dried apricots, diced or thin sliced
- ½ cup dried figs, diced or thinly sliced
- Pinch salt

Method

1. Combine the olive oil, maple syrup, vanilla, cardamom, and allspice in a large sauté pan over medium heat. Stir to combine.
2. Add the nuts and seeds and stir well to coat. Let the nuts and seeds toast for about 10 minutes, stirring frequently.
3. Remove from the heat, and add the dried apricots and figs. Stir everything well and season with salt.
4. Store in an airtight container.

Per Serving:

Calories: 261; Fat: 18g; Carbs: 23g; Protein: 6g

169. Seared Halloumi with Pesto and Tomato

Time: 5 minutes | Serves 2

Ingredients:

- 3 ounces Halloumi cheese, cut crosswise into 2 thinner, rectangular pieces
- 2 teaspoons prepared pesto sauce, plus additional for drizzling if desired
- 1 medium tomato, sliced

Method

1. Heat a nonstick skillet over medium-high heat and place the slices of Halloumi in the hot pan.
2. After about 2 minutes, check to see if the cheese is golden on the bottom.
3. If it is, flip the slices, top each with 1 teaspoon of pesto, and cook for another 2 minutes, or until the second side is golden.
4. Serve with slices of tomato and a drizzle of pesto, if desired, on the side.

Per Serving:

Calories: 177; Fat: 14g; Carbs: 4g; Protein: 10g

170. Stuffed Cucumber Cups

Time: 5 minutes | Serves 2

Ingredients:

- 1 medium cucumber (about 8 ounces, 8 to 9 inches long)
- ½ cup hummus (any flavor) or white bean dip
- 4 or 5 cherry tomatoes, sliced in half
- 2 tablespoons fresh basil, minced

Method

1. Slice the ends off the cucumber (about ½ inch from each side) and slice the cucumber into 1-inch pieces.
2. With a paring knife or a spoon, scoop most of the seeds from the inside of each cucumber piece to make a cup, being careful to not cut all the way through.
3. Fill each cucumber cup with about 1 tablespoon of hummus or bean dip.
4. Top each with a cherry tomato half and a sprinkle of fresh minced basil.

Per Serving:

Calories: 135; fat: 6g; carbs: 16g; Protein: 6g

171.   Apple Chips with Chocolate Tahini

Time: 10 minutes | Serves 2

Ingredients:

- 2 tablespoons tahini
- 1 tablespoon maple syrup
- 1 tablespoon unsweetened cocoa powder
- 1 to 2 tablespoons warm water (or more if needed)
- 2 medium apples
- 1 tablespoon roasted, salted sunflower seeds

Method

1. In a small bowl, mix together the tahini, maple syrup, and cocoa powder. Add warm water, a little at a time, until thin enough to drizzle. Do not microwave it to thin it—it won't work.
2. Slice the apples crosswise into round slices, and then cut each piece in half to make a chip.
3. Lay the apple chips out on a plate and drizzle them with the chocolate tahini sauce.
4. Sprinkle sunflower seeds over the apple chips.

Per Serving:

Calories: 261; fat: 11g; carbs: 43g; Protein: 5g

172.   Strawberry Caprese Skewers

Time: 15 minutes | Serves 2

Ingredients:

- ½ cup balsamic vinegar
- 16 whole, hulled strawberries
- 12 small basil leaves or 6 large leaves, halved
- 12 pieces of small mozzarella balls (ciliegine)

Method

1. To make the balsamic glaze, pour the balsamic vinegar into a small saucepan and bring it to a boil.
2. Reduce the heat to medium-low and simmer for 10 minutes, or until it's reduced by half and is thick enough to coat the back of a spoon.
3. On each of 4 wooden skewers, place a strawberry, a folded basil leaf, and a mozzarella ball, repeating twice and adding a strawberry on the end. (Each skewer should have 4 strawberries, 3 basil leaves, and 3 mozzarella balls.)
4. Drizzle 1 to 2 teaspoons of balsamic glaze over the skewers.

Per Serving:

Calories: 206; fat: 10g; carbs: 17g; Protein: 10g

173.   Herbed Labneh Vegetable Parfaits

Time: 15 minutes | Serves 2

Ingredients:

For the labneh

- 8 ounces plain Greek yogurt (full-fat works best)
- Generous pinch salt
- 1 teaspoon za'atar seasoning
- 1 teaspoon freshly squeezed lemon juice
- Pinch lemon zest

For the parfaits

- ½ cup peeled, chopped cucumber
- ½ cup grated carrots
- ½ cup cherry tomatoes, halved

Method

1. Line a strainer with cheesecloth and place it over a bowl.
2. Stir together the Greek yogurt and salt and place in the cheesecloth. Wrap it up and let it sit for 24 hours in the refrigerator.
3. When ready, unwrap the labneh and place it into a clean bowl. Stir in the za'atar, lemon juice, and lemon zest.
4. Divide the cucumber between two clear glasses.
5. Top each portion of cucumber with about 3 tablespoons of labneh. Divide the carrots between the glasses.
6. Top with another 3 tablespoons of the labneh. Top parfaits with the cherry tomatoes.

Per Serving:

Calories: 143; Fat: 7g; Carbs: 16g; Protein: 5g

174.   Fool-Proof Hummus

Time: 10 minutes | Serves 2

Ingredients:

- 1 (15-ounce) can chickpeas
- 2 tablespoons of liquid reserved before draining from the can of chickpeas
- ¼ cup tahini sauce

- 2 tablespoons olive oil
- Juice from 1 lemon
- 1 garlic clove, minced
- ½ teaspoon ground cumin
- Salt and pepper, to taste

Method

1. Add all the ingredients to a food processor.
2. Pulse until creamy.
3. Serve with toasted bread or diced veggies.

Per Serving:

Calories 562, Fat 32g, Carbs 57g, Protein 16 G

175.   Pea and Avocado Guacamole

Time: 10 minutes | Serves 2

Ingredients:

- ½ cup frozen peas, thawed
- 2 ripe avocados, pitted, peeled, and diced
- Juice of 1 lemon
- ½ red onion, diced
- Pinch of smoked paprika
- Salt and pepper, to taste

Method

1. In a food processor, place the peas, avocado, lemon juice, red onion, smoked paprika, salt, and pepper. Pulse until creamy.
2. Serve with tortilla chips, crackers, breadsticks, or vegetables.

Per Serving:

Calories 453, fat 39 g, carbs 25 g, Protein 6 g

176.   Caprese Skewers

Time: 15 minutes | Serves 2

Ingredients:

- 36 cherry tomatoes

- 24 mini mozzarella balls
- 36 fresh basil leaves
- 1 tablespoon extra-virgin olive oil
- 1 teaspoon Italian seasoning
- 1 tablespoon balsamic glaze
- Salt and pepper, to taste

Method

1. Prepare the skewers by threading one cherry tomato, one mini mozzarella ball, and one basil leaf onto each skewer.
2. Repeat until all skewers have been assembled. In a small bowl, mix together the olive oil, Italian seasoning, salt, and pepper.
3. To create a well-blended mixture, use a whisk to thoroughly combine the ingredients until they are fully incorporated.
4. Ensure that all the components are evenly mixed together. Ensure that all components are thoroughly integrated for optimal taste.
5. Drizzle the olive oil mixture over the assembled skewers. Drizzle the balsamic glaze over the skewers.
6. Serve the caprese skewers immediately as an appetizer or a light snack.

Per Serving

Calories: 150 kcal, Fat: 10 g Carbs: 6 g, Protein: 9 g

177.   Mini Quesadillas

Time: 10 minutes | Serves 2

Ingredients:

- 8 small flour tortillas
- 1 cup shredded cheese (cheddar, Monterey Jack, or a blend)

Optional fillings:

- Diced Cooked Chicken
- Sautéed Vegetables
- Black Beans
- Corn

Optional garnishes:

- Sour Cream
- Salsa
- Guacamole
- Cilantro

Method

1. To prepare for cooking, make sure to preheat the skillet or griddle over medium heat. This step is essential for achieving optimal cooking results.
2. Place a tortilla onto the skillet and evenly spread shredded cheese on a single side of the tortilla. Should you desire, you have the option to add extra fillings on the layer of cheese.
3. Gently press down with a spatula to fold the tortilla in half, ensuring that the edges are sealed. Cook each side of the tortilla for around 2-3 minutes, or until it achieves a golden brown color and the cheese has fully melted.
4. Take out the quesadilla from the skillet and proceed to repeat the same process with the remaining tortillas and fillings.
5. Cut each cooked quesadilla into quarters to create mini quesadillas. Serve the mini quesadillas warm with your choice of garnishes.

Per Serving

Calories: 300 kcal, Fat: 12 g, Carbs: 35 g, Protein: 12 g

178.   Greek Yogurt Parfait

Time: 10 minutes | Serves 2

Ingredients:

- 2 cups plain Greek yogurt
- 1 cup fresh berries (strawberries, blueberries, raspberries)
- ½ cup granola

Optional:

- Honey or maple syrup for drizzling

Method

1. In serving glasses or bowls, layer 1/4 cup of Greek yogurt at the bottom.
2. Place a generous layer of fresh berries on the surface of the yogurt.
3. If you prefer a sweeter taste, you have the option to drizzle honey or maple syrup over the top of the dish, providing an additional touch of sweetness.
4. Repeat the layers with another 1/4 cup of Greek yogurt, more berries, and granola.
5. If desired, enhance the sweetness by drizzling honey or maple syrup over the top.
6. Repeat the layering process for the remaining glasses or bowls. Serve the Greek yogurt parfaits immediately or refrigerate until ready to serve.

Per Serving:

Calories: 200 kcal, Fat: 4 g, Carbs: 25 g, Protein: 18 g

179.   Bruschetta

Time: 15 minutes | Serves 2

Ingredients:

- 4 slices of crusty bread (baguette or Italian bread)
- 2 ripe tomatoes, diced

- ¼ cup fresh basil leaves, chopped
- 2 cloves garlic, minced
- 2 tablespoons extra-virgin olive oil
- 1 tablespoon balsamic vinegar
- Salt and pepper, to taste

Method

1. Preheat the broiler in your oven. In a bowl, combine the diced tomatoes, chopped basil, minced garlic, olive oil, balsamic vinegar, salt, and pepper. Mix well to combine all the ingredients. Position the bread slices on a baking sheet and transfer them to the broiler.
2. Toast each side for about 2-3 minutes, or until they achieve a desired golden brown hue and a crispy texture.
3. Once the bread is toasted, carefully remove it from the oven and let it cool for a short while before handling. Spoon the tomato and basil mixture onto each bread slice, spreading it evenly.
4. Present the bruschetta promptly, either as an appetizer or a light snack, for immediate enjoyment.

Per Serving:

Calories: 170 kcal, Fat: 8 g, Carbs: 20 g, Protein: 4 g

180.   Smashed Avocado Toast

Time: 10 minutes | Serves 2

Ingredients:

1. 1 small avocado 1 teaspoon fresh lemon juice
2. ¼ teaspoon Kosher salt
3. ¼ teaspoon freshly ground black pepper
4. 1 slice whole grain bread, toasted
5. 1 teaspoon extra-virgin olive oil
6. Optional garnish:
7. Maldon sea salt flakes or red pepper flakes

Method

1. In a small bowl, combine the avocado, lemon juice, salt, and pepper.
2. Utilizing the back of a fork, apply gentle pressure and mash the avocado until it reaches the consistency that suits your preference.
3. Spread the mashed avocado mixture evenly on the toasted bread.
4. Drizzle the olive oil over the avocado. Sprinkle with desired garnish, such as Maldon sea salt flakes or red pepper flakes.
5. Serve the smashed avocado toast immediately.

Per Serving:

Calories: 200 kcal, Fat: 13 g, Carbs: 18 g, Protein: 5 g

Desserts:

181. Strawberries with Balsamic Vinegar

Time: 5 minutes | Serves 2

Ingredients:

- 2 cups strawberries, hulled and sliced
- 2 tablespoons sugar
- 2 tablespoons balsamic vinegar

Method

1. Place the sliced strawberries in a bowl, sprinkle with the sugar, and drizzle lightly with the balsamic vinegar.
2. Toss to combine well and allow to sit for about 10 minutes before serving.

Per Serving

Calories: 92, Fat: 0.4g, Carbs: 21.7g, Protein: 1.0g

182. Frozen Mango Raspberry

Time: 5 minutes | Serves 2

Ingredients:

- 3 cups frozen raspberries
- 1 mango, peeled and pitted
- 1 peach, peeled and pitted
- 1 teaspoon honey

Method

1. Place all the ingredients into a blender and purée, adding some water as needed.
2. Put in the freezer for 10 minutes to firm up if desired.
3. Serve chilled or at room temperature.

183.   Grilled Stone Fruit with Honey

Time: 14 minutes | Serves 2

Ingredients:

- 3 apricots, halved and pitted
- 2 plums, halved and pitted
- 2 peaches, halved and pitted
- ½ cup low-fat ricotta cheese
- 2 tablespoons honey
- Cooking spray

Method

1. Preheat the grill to medium heat.
2. Spray the grill grates with cooking spray.
3. Arrange the fruit, cut side down, on the grill, and cook for 2 to 3 minutes per side, or until lightly charred and softened.
4. Serve warm with a sprinkle of cheese and a drizzle of honey.

Per Serving

calories: 298, fat: 7.8g, carbs: 45.2g, protein: 11.9g

184.   Orange Mug Cakes

Time: 13 minutes | Serves 2

Ingredients:

- 6 tablespoons flour
- 2 tablespoons sugar

- 1 teaspoon orange zest
- ½ teaspoon baking powder
- Pinch salt
- 1 egg
- 2 tablespoons olive oil
- 2 tablespoons unsweetened almond milk
- 2 tablespoons freshly squeezed orange juice
- ½ teaspoon orange extract
- ½ teaspoon vanilla extract

Method

1. Combine the flour, sugar, orange zest, baking powder, and Salt in a small bowl.
2. In another bowl, whisk together the egg, olive oil, milk, orange juice, orange extract, and vanilla extract.
3. Add the dry ingredients to the wet ingredients and stir to incorporate. The batter will be thick.
4. Divide the mixture into two small mugs. Microwave each mug separately.
5. The small ones should take about 60 seconds, and one large mug should take about 90 seconds, but microwaves can vary. Cool for 5 minutes before serving.

Per Serving

Calories: 303, Fat: 16.9g, Carbs: 32.5g, Protein: 6.0g

185.   Fruit and Nut Chocolate Bark

Time: 15 minutes | Serves 2

Ingredients:

- 2 tablespoons chopped nuts
- 3 ounces' dark chocolate chips
- ¼ cup chopped dried fruit (blueberries, apricots, figs, prunes, or any combination of those)

Method

1. Line a sheet pan with parchment paper and set aside. Add the nuts to a skillet over medium-high heat and toast for 60 seconds, or just fragrant. Set aside to cool.
2. Put the chocolate chips in a microwave-safe glass bowl and microwave on High for 1 minute.
3. Stir the chocolate and allow any unmelted chips to warm and melt. If desired, heat for an additional 20 to 30 seconds.
4. Transfer the chocolate to the prepared sheet pan. Scatter the dried fruit and toasted nuts over the chocolate evenly and gently pat in so they stick.
5. Place the sheet pan in the refrigerator for at least 1 hour to let the chocolate harden. When ready, break into pieces and serve.

Per Serving

Calories: 285, Fat: 16.1g, Carbs: 38.7g, Protein: 4.0g

186.　　Cozy Superfood Hot Chocolate

Time: 13 minutes | Serves 2

Ingredients:

- 2 cups unsweetened almond milk
- 1 tablespoon avocado oil
- 1 tablespoon collagen protein powder
- 2 teaspoons coconut sugar
- 2 tablespoons cocoa powder
- 1 teaspoon ground cinnamon
- 1 teaspoon ground ginger
- 1 teaspoon vanilla extract
- ½ teaspoon ground turmeric
- Dash salt Dash cayenne pepper (optional)

Method

1. In a small saucepan over medium heat, warm the almond milk and avocado oil for about 7 minutes, stirring frequently.
2. Fold in the protein powder, which will only properly dissolve in a heated liquid.
3. Stir in the coconut sugar and cocoa powder until melted and dissolved.
4. Carefully transfer the warm liquid into a blender, along with the cinnamon, ginger, vanilla, turmeric, salt, and cayenne pepper (if desired).
5. Blend for 15 seconds until frothy. Serve immediately.

Per Serving

Calories: 217, Fat: 11.0g, 14.8g, Protein: 11. 2g Carbs

187.   Spicy Hot Chocolate

Time: 10 minutes | Serves 2

Ingredients:

- ¼ tsp cayenne pepper powder
- 2 squares semisweet chocolate
- 2 cups milk
- 1 tsp sugar
- ¼ tsp ground cinnamon
- ¼ tsp salt

Method

1. Place milk and sugar in a pot over low heat and warm until it simmers.
2. Combine dark chocolate, cinnamon, salt, and cayenne pepper powder in a bowl. Slowly pour in enough hot milk to cover.
3. Return the pot to the heat and lower the temperature.
4. Mix until the chocolate has melted, then combine the remaining milk.
5. Spoon into 2 cups and serve hot.

Per Serving:

Calories: 342, Fat: 23g, Carbs: 22g, Protein: 12g

188.   Fruit Cups with Orange Juice

Time: 10 minutes | Serves 2

Ingredients:

- 1 cup orange juice
- ½ cup watermelon cubes
- 1 ½ cups grapes, halved
- 1 cup chopped cantaloupe
- ½ cup cherries, pitted and chopped
- 1 peach, chopped
- ½ tsp ground cinnamon

Method

1. Combine watermelon cubes, grapes, cherries, cantaloupe, and peach in a bowl.
2. Add the juice of an orange and mix well.
3. Share into dessert cups, dust with cinnamon, and serve chilled.

Per Serving:

Calories: 156, Fat: 0.5g, Carbs: 24.2g, Protein: 1.8g

189.   Strawberry & Cocoa Yogurt

Time: 5 minutes | Serves 2

Ingredients:

- ¾ cup Greek yogurt
- 1 tbsp. cocoa powder
- ¼ cup strawberries, chopped
- 5 drops vanilla stevia

Method

1. Combine cocoa powder, strawberries, yogurt, and stevia in a bowl.
2. Serve immediately.

Per Serving:

Calories: 210, Fat: 9g, Carbs: 8g, Protein: 5g

190.   Raspberries & Lime Frozen Yogurt

Time: 10 minutes | Serves 2

Ingredients:

- 1 cup fresh raspberries
- 2 cups vanilla frozen yogurt
- 1 lime, zested
- ¼ cup chopped praline pecans

Method

1. Divide the frozen yogurt into 4 dessert glasses.
2. Top with raspberries, lime zest, and pecans.
3. Serve immediately.

Per Serving:

Calories: 142, Fat: 3.4g, Carbs: 26.2g, Protein: 3.7g

191.   Maple Grilled Pineapple

Time: 15 minutes | Serves 2

Ingredients:

- 1 tbsp. maple syrup
- 1 pineapple, peeled and cut into wedges
- ½ tsp ground cinnamon

Method

1. Preheat a grill pan over high heat.
2. Drizzle the fruit in a bowl with maple syrup; sprinkle with ground cinnamon.
3. Grill for about 7-8 minutes, occasionally turning until the fruit chars slightly.
4. Serve and enjoy.

Per Serving:

Calories: 120, Fat: 1g, Carbs: 33g, Protein: 1g

192.   Yogurt and Berry Tiramisu

Time: 15 minutes | Serves 2

Ingredients:

- ¾ cup desired berries, fresh
- 4 small sponge cupcakes, vanilla flavored, low-fat
- 1 tablespoon brown sugar
- 3 tablespoon cocoa powder, unsweetened
- ½ teaspoon vanilla extract, unsweetened
- 1 cup yogurt, low-fat
- 2 tablespoon blueberry juice, unsweetened
- ¼ cup water

Method

1. Take a small pot, place it over low heat, add ¼ cup berries and sugar, pour in the water, and then cook for 5 minutes or more until the sugar has melted.
2. Then remove the pot from heat and let it cool at room temperature.
3. Take a large bowl, place yogurt in it, vanilla extract, and stir until well blended.
4. Take a serving glass, place two cupcakes in it and then top with one-fourth of the prepared berry mixture.
5. Layer the berry mixture with the prepared yogurt mixture, sprinkle with half of the cocoa powder, and then layer it with one-fourth of the prepared berry mixture.

6. Assemble another parfait glass in the same manner and then serve.

Per Serving

Calories: 220; Fat: 1g; Carbs: 41.3g; Protein: 4g

193.   Strawberry and Avocado Medley

Time: 5 minutes | Serves 2

Ingredients:

- 1 cup strawberry, halved
- ½ avocado, pitted and sliced
- 1 tablespoon slivered almonds

Method

1. Place all ingredients in a mixing bowl.
2. Toss to combine. Allow chilling in the fridge before serving.

Per Serving:

Calories: 107; Fat: 7.8g; Carbs: 9.9g; Protein: 1.6g

194.   No Bake Mosaic Cake

Time: 10 minutes | Serves 2

Ingredients:

- ½ lb. petit Beurre biscuits, broken into squares and put aside
- ½ cup of sugar
- ½ cup of cocoa powder
- 1teaspoon vanilla extract
- 2 eggs
- ½ cup of butter, melted
- 2oz of dark chocolate, melted

Method

1. Mix butter with chocolate in a bowl. Combine sugar with vanilla extract and cocoa powder in another bowl
2. Add butter and chocolate mixture to the bowl and mix well. Whisk in eggs and beat until thick and creamy.
3. Fold in broken biscuit pieces to the batter. Transfer this batter to a loaf pan lined with plastic wrap.
4. Fold the wrap to cover the batter and refrigerate for 3 hrs. Or more.
5. Slice and serve

Per Serving:

Calories 850, Fat 47.8g, Carbs 100.5g, Protein 13.2g

195.   Chocolate pudding

Time: 5 minutes | Serves 2

Ingredients:

- 2 tsp extract of vanilla
- 1/3 cup raw cacao powder
- 1 avocado large, chilled
- ½ cup full fat coconut milk
- 1/3 cup maple syrup

Method

1. Take the avocados and slice them in half. Then you will need to remove the pit.
2. You will now need to scoop the flesh out and put it in a food processor.
3. Add in the rest of the Ingredients: and make sure you blend until its creamy.
4. Serve with toppings if desired.

Per Serving:

Calories 295.3, Fat 20.9g, Carbs 29.1g, Protein 3.4g

196.   Greek yogurt bowl

Time: 5 minutes | Serves 2

Ingredients:

- ¼ cup natural and creamy peanut butter
- 1 cup Greek vanilla yogurt
- ¼ cup flax seed meal
- 1 tsp nutmeg
- 1 medium sliced banana

Method

1. Split the yogurt into the bowls and top with bananas.
2. Melt the peanut butter in the microwave for a maximum of 40 seconds.
3. Drizzle it over each bowl.
4. Place the nutmeg and flaxseed over the top.

Per Serving:

Calories 370, Fat 10.6g, Carbs 47.7g, Protein 22.7g

197.   Yogurt Parfait with Granola

Time: 10 minutes | Serves 2

Ingredients:

- 1 cup Greek yogurt
- 1/2 cup granola
- 1/2 cup pomegranate seeds
- 1 tablespoon honey (optional)
- A pinch of cinnamon (optional

Method

1. Divide the Greek yogurt between two glasses or bowls.
2. Layer each with granola and pomegranate seeds.
3. Drizzle honey over each parfait and sprinkle with a pinch of cinnamon if desired.
4. Serve immediately or chill until ready to serve.

Per Serving

Calories: 250, Protein: 12g, Carbs: 36g, Fat: 7g

198.   Saffron and Cardamom Ice Cream

Time: 10 minutes | Serves 2

Ingredients:

- A pinch of saffron strands
- 1 cup heavy cream
- 1/2 cup whole milk
- 1/4 cup sugar
- 4 cardamom pods, crushed
- 2 egg yolks

Method

1. Soak the saffron strands in 2 tablespoons of warm milk in a small bowl for 10 minutes.
2. Combine heavy cream, milk, sugar, and cardamom pods in a saucepan.
3. Heat over medium until sugar dissolves and the mixture is hot, not boiling. Whisk egg yolks in a separate bowl.
4. Gradually add a bit of the hot milk mixture to the yolks, stirring constantly. Pour the yolk mixture back into the saucepan.
5. Cook on low heat, stirring until the mixture thickens enough to coat the back of a spoon.
6. Strain the mixture, add the saffron milk, and calm it down. Freeze according to your ice cream maker's instructions.

199.   Orange Olive Oil Mug Cakes

Time: 12 minutes | Serves 2

Ingredients:

- 6 tablespoons flour
- 2 tablespoons sugar
- ½ teaspoon baking powder
- Pinch salt
- 1 teaspoon orange zest
- 1 egg
- 2 tablespoons olive oil
- 2 tablespoons freshly squeezed orange juice
- 2 tablespoons milk
- ½ teaspoon orange extract
- ½ teaspoon vanilla extract

Method

1. In a small bowl, combine the flour, sugar, baking powder, salt, and orange zest.
2. In a separate bowl, whisk together the egg, olive oil, orange juice, milk, orange extract, and vanilla extract.
3. Pour the dry ingredients into the wet ingredients and stir to combine. The batter will be thick.
4. Divide the mixture into two small mugs that hold at least 6 ounces each, or one 12-ounce mug.
5. Microwave each mug separately. The small ones should take about 60 seconds, and one large mug should take about 90 seconds, but microwaves can vary. The cake will be done when it pulls away from the sides of the mug.

Per Serving:

Calories: 302; Fat: 17g; Carbs: 33g; Protein: 6g

200. Dark Chocolate Bark with Fruit and Nuts

Time: 15 minutes | Serves 2

Ingredients:

- 2 tablespoons chopped nuts (almonds, pecans, walnuts, hazelnuts, pistachios, or any combination of those)
- 3 ounces good-quality dark chocolate chips (about ⅔ cup)
- ¼ cup chopped dried fruit (apricots, blueberries, figs, prunes, or any combination of those)

Method

1. Line a sheet pan with parchment paper. Place the nuts in a skillet over medium-high heat and toast them for 60 seconds, or just until they're fragrant.
2. Place the chocolate in a microwave-safe glass bowl or measuring cup and microwave on high for 1 minute. Stir the chocolate and allow any unmelted chips to warm and melt. If necessary, heat for another 20 to 30 seconds, but keep a close eye on it to make sure it doesn't burn.
3. Pour the chocolate onto the sheet pan. Sprinkle the dried fruit and nuts over the chocolate evenly and gently pat in so they stick.
4. Transfer the sheet pan to the refrigerator for at least 1 hour to let the chocolate harden.
5. When solid, break into pieces. Store any leftover chocolate in the refrigerator or freezer.

Per Serving:

Calories: 284; Fat: 16g; Carbs: 39g; Protein: 4g

Appendix: Conversions & Equivalents

Volume Equivalents (Liquid)		
Standard	Us Standard (Ounces)	Metric (Approximate)
2 tablespoons	1 fl. oz.	30 mL
¼ cup	2 fl. oz.	60 mL
½ cup	4 fl. oz.	120 mL
1 cup	8 fl. oz.	240 mL
1½ cups	12 fl. oz.	355 mL
2 cups or 1 pint	16 fl. oz.	475 mL
4 cups or 1 quart	32 fl. oz.	1 L
1 gallon	128 fl.	oz. 4 L

Oven Temperatures	
Fahrenheit (F)	Celsius (C) (Approximate)
250°	120°
300°	150°
325°	165°
350°	180°
375°	190°
400°	200°
425°	220°
450°	230°

Volume Equivalents (Dry)	
Standard	**Metric (Approximate)**
⅛ teaspoon	0.5 mL
¼ teaspoon	1 mL
½ teaspoon	2 mL
¾ teaspoon	4 mL
1 teaspoon	5 mL
1 tablespoon	15 mL
¼ cup	59 mL
⅓ cup	79 mL
½ cup	118 mL
⅔ cup	156 mL
¾ cup	177 mL
1 cup	235 mL
2 cups or 1 pint	475 mL
3 cups	700 mL
4 cups or 1 quart	1 L

Weight Equivalents	
Standard	**Metric (Approximate)**
½ ounce	15 g
1 ounce	30 g
2 ounces	60 g
4 ounces	115 g
8 ounces	225 g
12 ounces	340 g
16 ounces or 1 pound	455 g

Appendix 2: Recipe Index

Almond Banana Pancakes	42
Apple Chips with Chocolate Tahini	186
Artichoke Crab	80
Artichoke Salad	94
Authentic Mediterranean Hummus	178
Avocado and Cucumber Salad	95
Baked Beet Chips	74
Baked Eggs with Avocado and Feta	40
Baked White Fish with Vegetables	170
Basil Artichoke	112
Basil Meatballs	147
Bean and Veggie Pasta	48
Beef & Eggplant Casserole	149
Beet and Carrot Fritters with Yogurt Sauce	99
Beet Hummus	76
Breakfast Pizza	31
Broccoli and Carrot Pasta Salad	48
Bruschetta	192
Bruschetta Chicken Burgers	129
Bruschetta with Tomato and Basil	35
Bulgur Pilaf with Kale and Tomatoes	50
Caprese Salad	96

Caprese Skewers	189
Catalan-Style Spinach	107
Cauliflower Rice	113
Chicken and Broccoli Salad	96
Chicken Bruschetta Burgers	118
Chicken Gyros with Tzatziki Sauce	119
Chicken Skillet with Mushrooms	121
Chicken Souvlaki	134
Chicken Wrap Tortilla Bread and Fried Chicken	36
Chickpea Soup with Pasta	83
Chili Broccoli	113
Chili-Garlic Rice with Halloumi	57
Chocolate pudding	205
Citrus Fennel Salad	88
Citrus Salad with Kale and Fennel	90
Classic Spaghetti Aglio E Olio	59
Couscous with Olives and Feta Cheese	71
Cozy Superfood Hot Chocolate	198
Cranberry and Almond Quinoa	51
Creamy Tomato Hummus Soup	82
Creole Spaghetti	58
Crispy Garlic Shrimp	168
Crusted Herb Pork Chops	150
Crusty Halibut	163
Cucumber and Tomato Salad	91
Cumin Quinoa Pilaf	52

Dark Chocolate Bark with Fruit and Nuts 208

Dill Chutney Salmon 172

Easy Pork Chops in Tomato Sauce 144

Easy Veggie Wrap 103

Eggplant Dip 79

Fennel Lamb Chops 145

Feta and Cheese Couscous 108

Feta Cheese Cubes with Herbs and Olives 180

Fig and Arugula Salad 86

Fool-Proof Hummus 188

Fried Spicy Shrimps 181

Frozen Mango Raspberry 195

Fruit and Nut Chocolate Bark 197

Fruit Cups with Orange Juice 200

Garlic & Lemon Sea Bass 167

Garlic Scallops 171

Garlic-Butter Parmesan Salmon and Asparagus 173

Ginger and Orange Rice 70

Greek Salad with Grilled Chicken 97

Greek Turkey Cutlets 136

Greek Turkey Meatballs 125

Greek yogurt bowl 205

Greek Yogurt Pancakes 39

Greek Yogurt Parfait 191

Greek-Style Ground Beef Pita Sandwiches 152

Greek-Style Lamb Burgers 144

Grilled Broccoli Rabe	68
Grilled Chicken Breasts with Spinach Pesto	122
Grilled Eggplant Salad	92
Grilled Eggplant Stacks	102
Grilled Eggplant with Basil and Parsley	110
Grilled Lamb Chops	140
Grilled Lemon Pesto Salmon	174
Grilled Octopus	161
Grilled Radicchio with Blue Cheese	69
Grilled Sardines on Toast	182
Grilled Stone Fruit with Honey	196
Hamburgers	142
Herbed Labneh Vegetable Parfaits	187
Hot and Fresh Fishy Steaks	166
Hot Chicken with Black Beans	127
Hummus	78
Hummus with Parsley and Pita	179
Italian Eggplant Sandwich	104
Italian Fried Calamari	73
Kofta Kebabs	139
Lamb Chops with Herb Butter	148
Lamb Meatballs with Tzatziki	146
Lemon and Paprika Herb-Marinated Chicken	131
Lemon Garlic Pasta	61
Lemon-Parsley Swordfish	160
Maple Grilled Pineapple	202

Mediterranean Chicken Salad Wraps   132

Mediterranean Chickpea Salad   177

Mediterranean Pinto Beans   55

Mediterranean Tomato Hummus Soup   82

Mediterranean Trail Mix   183

Mediterranean-Style Beans and Greens   47

Mini Quesadillas   190

Miso Soup   86

Mixed Salad with Balsamic Honey Dressing   89

Mixed Vegetable Pasta   53

Moroccan-Style Couscous   67

Mushroom Salad with Blue Cheese and Arugula   93

Mussels O' Marine   165

Nettle Soup   84

No Bake Mosaic Cake   204

Omelette with Spinach and Cheese   34

One-Pot Chicken Pesto Pasta   135

Orange Cardamom Buckwheat Pancakes   29

Orange Mug Cakes   196

Orange Olive Oil Mug Cakes   207

Orzo with Herbs   111

Overnight Pomegranate Muesli   30

Pan-Seared Pork Chops   141

Parmesan Omelet   42

Pasta and Chickpea Soup   60

Pasta with Cashew Sauce   46

Pea and Avocado Guacamole 189

Peach Caprese Skewers 78

Pear Salad with Roquefort Cheese 91

Pesto Fish Fillet 158

Pesto Pasta 62

Pork Chops in Wine Sauce 139

Pork Souvlaki Pita 154

Power Peach Smoothie Bowl 32

Quesadillas 44

Quick Hummus Bowls 103

Raspberries & Lime Frozen Yogurt 201

Roasted Broccolini with Garlic and Romano 65

Roasted Chickpeas 73

Roasted Garlicky Kale 69

Roasted Pumpkin Seeds 75

Roasted Zucchini 72

Saffron and Cardamom Ice Cream 207

Sage Pork Chops with Sweet & Spicy Chutney 156

Salmon and Mango Mix 158

Salmon with Vegetables 169

Sausages with Vegetables 138

Sautéed Spinach and Leeks 115

Seared Halloumi with Pesto and Tomato 184

Sicilian Olive Chicken 120

Simple Honey-Glazed Baby Carrots 116

Simple Sautéed Cauliflower 108

Smashed Avocado Toast   193

Smokey Glazed Tuna   164

Socca Pan Pizza with Herbed Ricotta, Fresh Tomato, And Balsamic Glaze   100

Spaghetti with Tuna and Capers   162

Spanish Cold Soup (Ajo Blanco)   85

Spiced Chicken Thighs with Saffron Basmati Rice   133

Spiced Chickpeas   56

Spiced Lamb and Beef Kebabs   155

Spicy Hot Chocolate   199

Spicy Lamb Burgers with Harissa Mayo   151

Spicy Wilted Greens with Garlic   65

Spinach and Egg Breakfast Wraps   41

Spinach, Sun-Dried Tomato, and Feta Egg Wraps   33

Spiralized Carrot with Peas   106

Squash and Zucchini Fritters   182

Steamed Trout with Lemon Herb Crust   175

Strawberries with Balsamic Vinegar   195

Strawberry & Cocoa Yogurt   201

Strawberry and Avocado Medley   203

Strawberry and Lemon Millet Bowl   37

Strawberry Basil Honey Ricotta Toast   30

Strawberry Caprese Skewers   186

Stuffed Cucumber Cups   185

Three Bean Mix   54

Thyme Pork Steak   148

Toasts with Avocado Cream Cheese   33

Tomato Basil Pasta 49

Tomato Stuffed with Cheese & Peppers 105

Tomato Tuna Melts 176

Trout and Tzatziki Sauce 159

Tuna & Rosemary Pizza 54

Tuna Salad Sandwiches 77

Turkey Patties 126

Turkey Pepperoni Pizza 128

Turkey with Rigatoni 124

Tuscan Style Chicken 124

Vanilla Pancakes 43

Vegan Carbonara 63

Vegetable & Chicken Skewers 123

Vegetable Cakes 109

Vegetable Frittata 36

Veggie Rice Bowls with Pesto Sauce 114

Watermelon Feta Salad 87

Whipped Feta and Olive Toasts 38

White Beans with Rosemary, Sage, And Garlic 66

Yogurt and Berry Tiramisu 202

Yogurt Parfait with Granola 206

Made in United States
Troutdale, OR
12/04/2024